D1076492

Super
MACHINE KNITS

Collins
8 Grafton Street,
London W1X 3LA

Super MACHINE KNITS

JUDY DODSON

COLLINS

First published in 1988 by
William Collins Sons & Co Ltd
London Glasgow Sydney
Auckland Toronto Johannesburg

Text © 1988 Judy Dodson
Garments design copyright © 1988 Judy Dodson
Copyright this volume © 1988 The Paul Press Ltd

All rights reserved. No part of this publication may be
reproduced, stored in a retrieval system, or transmitted
in any form or by any means, electronic, mechanical,
photocopy recording or otherwise, without the prior
permission of the copyright holder.

British Library Cataloguing in Publication Data

Dodson, Judy
    Super machine knits.
    1. Knitting, machine   2. knitting Patterns
    I. Title
    746.43'2041   TT687

    ISBN 0-00-412271-2

Typeset by AKM Associates (UK) Ltd, Ajmal House,
Hayes Road, Southall, London UB2 5NG

Separated, printed and bound in Singapore through
Print Buyers' Database

This book was edited, designed and produced by
The Paul Press Ltd
41 - 42 Berners Street, London W1P 3AA

Editors	Emma Warlow
	Lynne Davies
Art Editor	Mike Snell
Designer	David Ayres
Art Assistant	Gary Scriven
Photography	Belinda Banks
Stylist	Amanda Cooke
Illustrations	Ian Bott
Art Director	Stephen McCurdy
Editorial Director	Jeremy Harwood

Please note that while we have exercised every care in the
compiling of these patterns, mistakes do sometimes
occur, and neither the author nor the publisher can
accept any responsibility for damage to materials or
machines which may occur, due to errors in printing.

CONTENTS

▌NTRODUCTION

When I first caught the machine knitting bug 15 years ago, I could hardly wait to get started. With pieces of the packaging cardboard still clinging to the sides of my brand new machine, I whizzed through my first garment in record time, to my immense satisfaction. In my haste to 'christen' my machine, I only read the sections of my instruction manual which were directly relevant to the simple jumper I had chosen to knit, as and when I found I needed them. This is not a practice that I would recommend, but it certainly opened my eyes to all the wonderful things that can be achieved using the most basic machine skills. I quickly learnt how to adapt those skills to great creative effect, without resorting to the manufacturers' techniques described in manuals such as weaving and tucking, which to this day I find rather unrewarding to use. My preference for simplicity, together with the fact that my Jones Lacemaker only had an eight button manual pattern selection (which made Fair Isle designs, for example, limited and time-consuming to execute), and my natural impatience, led me to experiment with short row working, ripples and ruched fabrics. Even though I now have access to a Knitmaster punchcard 323, and own a Brother chunky punchcard, I still prefer to spend time creating detail within a design, rather than simply punching out a card and leaving the work up to the machine. I hope my philosophy is reflected in the style of the designs in this book. I have tried hard to show a variety of different techniques within the designs, which might inspire you to create your own designs, if you don't want to follow my patterns exactly.

Machine knitting has only just begun to be recognized as a potentially exciting medium for design, having been sorely neglected for many years. But even now it is rare to see a feature on machine knitting in glossy women's magazines, whereas hand-knitting is featured regularly. This may be because there have been few designs for machine knitting that can compete with the style and quality of the intricate and lovely hand-knit patterns that are now available. I know myself just how exciting and stylish machine knits can be and it was my wish to promote them that motivated me to write this book. Just as Patricia Roberts changed our conception of the hand-knitted image, with her imaginative, complex and fashionable designs that appeal to young and old alike, I hope that this book will be a forerunner of many which confirm that machine knitting can challenge the monopoly of hand-knitting in the fashion world.

SIMPLICITY ITSELF
You do not have to rely on highly technical equipment to create stylish machine knit garments. I have taken great care to ensure that my designs can be knitted on any kind of machine. The patterns in this book have been designed for standard gauge machines, with punchcards and without, and chunky machines, again, with punchcards and without. A ribbing attachment has only been used for the welts, cuffs, or neck and button bands, which can all be worked by hand if necessary. I deliberately avoided using a ribber for racking, rib jacquards, or ripple fabrics, because I did not want to limit those knitters who do not have ribbing attachments. By the same token, I have not used garter carriages, or included patterns which are only suitable for 40 or 60 stitch electronic machines. You will see from the chart on page 16 that there are plenty of exciting designs which can be made on the most basic machines.

All the patterns should be used in conjunction with your machine manual. Even though the patterns have been written with the beginner in mind, a good working knowledge of your machine is invaluable if you are to work through the patterns without difficulty. Whether you are a novice or an experienced knitter, you will find that mishaps will sometimes occur in machine knitting, so do not feel discouraged. Start with a pattern with which you feel confident and take it slowly. I know that for many people the speed at which you can produce a garment on a knitting machine is the primary attraction, but spending a little more time on these patterns will produce a really professional end result – a designer garment that will rank with the most exquisite hand-knits.

THE PERFECT COMBINATION
Colour selection is possibly the most crucial part of the knitting process; it is as important as the choice of the pattern. I spend hours pondering

over different colour combinations to see which one will most enhance my design. A simple pullover in a good shape, worked in a natural fibre and superb colours will always look marvellous. Choosing the colours for a garment can be great fun and is a real creative challenge to enjoy.

It is all too easy when faced with a striking colour combination in a knitting design to play safe and stick to the shades of yarn used by the designer. Many knitters feel that they cannot possibly choose their own colours, especially when the choice available nowadays is so overwhelmingly wide. Walking into a wool shop fully stocked with hundreds of colourful yarns can be a very confusing experience, but with a little thought and experimentation beforehand, you should be able to select exactly the right combination to suit you and make the most of the design you want to knit up.

Several factors have to be taken into consideration when making your selection, including the colouring and tastes of the person for whom the garment is intended; the type of yarn you are going to use; and the visual impact of certain colour mixes. The first two considerations are obviously particular to specific knitting projects, but the latter is important for every single garment you create. The best way to develop a reliable colour sense is to collect a variety of appropriate reference material. Professional designers have substantial collections which they refer to time and time again in their work.

To begin with, why not have a browse through a furnishing fabric department? Textile designers have had years of practice co-ordinating colours successfully in different design contexts, and there is no reason why you should not benefit from their expertise. You can buy small sample pieces of the designs that particularly appeal to you to start your colour reference file. Wallpaper designs are another useful source of co-ordination ideas, as are paint shade charts. You should collect any magazine pictures that show unusual colour combinations in room settings, carpets or clothing – if you do not keep the pictures you will forget exactly how the colours worked together.

Armed with all your background work, take a trip to a good wool shop and try placing one colour strand of yarn next to another; this can help you decide whether or not a certain combination is effective. The marriage of some unexpected colour partners can be surprisingly illuminating. You may well find that particular shades of red look wonderful with bright pink or orange: a clashing combination you may previously have dismissed as harsh or tasteless. It is not only contrasting colours that produce unusual design effects; different textures of yarn

ABBREVIATIONS

WY	Waste Yarn
WP	Working Position
K	Knit
P	Purl
TD	Tension Dial
MT	Main Tension
MT -1	Tension Dial is set one whole number lower than main tension. eg. MT -2: set tension dial two whole numbers lower than main tension.
RC	Row Counter
R/S	Right Side
W/S	Wrong Side
L	Left
R	Right
MC	Main Colour
HP	Holding Position
NWP	Non-Working Position
rep	repeat
beg	beginning
st(s)	stitch(es)
rem	remaining
dec	decreas(e)(ing)
inc	increas(e)(ing)
foll	following
cont	continu(e)(ing)
carr	carriage
alt	alternate
ndl(s)	needle(s)
patt	pattern
cm	centimetre(s)
in	inch(es)
opp	opposite
tog	together
K/S	Knit Side
P/S	Purl Side
[ ]	Repeat section in brackets as stated. Figures in round brackets ( ) refer to larger sizes. Where only one set of figures is given this applies to all sizes.

can change the appearance of simple garments in very appealing ways.

The strength of the colour of a ball of yarn is far greater than the intensity of that same colour when it is combined with others in a garment. Every colour reacts and changes according to the colour next to it: an acid yellow for instance, will lose a great deal of its sharpness when mixed in small amounts with royal blue. Such a yellow can look rather overpowering by itself, but will be reduced so that it acts as a complimentary flash of contrast when it is immersed in the strong blue. A foolproof way of discovering the true compatability of certain colours is to knit a long strip, using up all the oddments you have to hand. With a punchcard unlocked, work 15 rows in main colour and contrast. Change main colour only and work a further 15 rows. Change contrast only and work another 15. Continue in this way and you will be amazed to see how some colours fade into insignificance while others seem to leap up at you from the knitting, proclaiming their superior impact. I have often discovered new colour combinations simply by muddling together balls of yarn in a variety of colours. As they are jumbled together, colours will suddenly land next to each other that look just right and a new colour combination is born. It can also be useful when you are doing this to stand back and look at the colours from a distance; you will be surprised at the difference some distance will make to the overall effect of the colourways.

A sense of colour *tones* is also important, not only for knitwear that incorporates several different shades, but also in single colour garments. There is no such thing as a single colour ▪ there are probably more than 30 tones of red available; some harsh and vibrant, others soft and more wearable. The tone of the colour you choose, together with the quality of the yarn, will determine the long life and continued appeal of any garment you knit. Colours belong in groups and work well if you mix them within their particular 'school' ▪ pastels, primaries, browns and greens. Mixing across the groups can be very effective ▪ try black, grey or cream with three bright primary colours, or three pastels. Or try brown, fawn and ecru with mustard, orange, turquoise or lilac. Do try to be adventurous with colour and add zest to your knitwear.

SELECTING YOUR YARN

The quality of the yarn you use will also radically affect the final appearance of your knitting. I feel that it is always more rewarding to use natural fibres; they may cost more than man-made yarns, but in the long run, your outlay will be more than repaid because garments made in natural yarns will always look good, 'hang' well and keep their shape. They may need to be washed with more care, but will generally need washing less often.

It is often said that beginners should use cheaper yarns for their first garments in case their work ends in disaster and the yarn is wasted, but I feel strongly that the reverse is true. The colours are better in good quality yarns, as is the texture, and I believe that knitters take more pride in their knitting as a result. They are also more likely to rectify mistakes and knit with more care if the yarn looks good and, as a result, they will probably end up with a garment they feel proud to own.

Machine knitters should not feel restricted to coned yarns alone. All too often, knitters send off to mail order firms for their yarn, having selected their colours from a shade card, only to be disappointed by the actual colours and texture of the yarns, which can take up to two or three weeks to be delivered. There is no reason why machine knitters should not be able to choose from the same extensive range of yarns available to hand-knitters, taking time to choose the right colours and buy exactly the right quantity. Owners of chunky machines have an even wider choice than most, as they can knit with knops, chenilles and mohairs.

Unfortunately, coned yarns are often only available in large amounts and machine knitters are left with all sorts of unused oddments of yarn. They are of course tempted to knit them all up together into a new garment, but this should really be avoided unless the oddments are of a uniform quality and in a sufficient variety of colours to ensure that the garment is excitingly multi-coloured. It is obviously far better to buy exactly the right amount of yarn for each garment you knit. You will notice that I have used standard balled yarns in many of the patterns in the book. It is really very easy to wind balled yarns ready for knitting on the machine. All you need to do is slightly flatten the ball, reach into the centre to locate the end of the yarn, and slip this end on to the wool-winder. Using the 'inner' end will prevent the ball from bouncing all over the floor as you wind! If this procedure does not appeal to you, however, many of the yarns featured come in manageable quantities, sometimes starting at cones of 250 g (9 oz).

Most of the spinners featured will have the qualities I have chosen available for up to two years. Then they will almost always replace their discontinued colours with similar matches, or alternatively bring in a whole new range of complementary colours to suit the season's fashions.

NOTES FOR NEW KNITTERS
Here are a few points of advice which may help the beginner:

1 Always have your manual handy, and work through all the techniques given, so that you have a good knowledge of your machine, and how to get out of trouble should you get into it!
2 Don't run before you can walk. Before starting any pattern in this book, read through it and if you come across a technique which you have not tried before, then experiment with some waste yarn until you are confident that you can manage it.
3 It can sometimes be a shock when you see a piece of work as it comes off the machine. I know just how disappointed beginners can be having seen how their work looks. Their first attempts at knitting may well have been dishearteningly tricky without the additional worry of seeing how messy the end result can be!

More experienced knitters know that with a little adjustment, all will be well. All work when it first comes off the machine is distorted widthways, so a good tug downwards will pull it into shape. This is especially important on chunky machines. Working neatly can also help to reduce the shabby appearance of a piece of knitting. Discard any waste yarn as you work. When introducing new colours, knit them into the end stitch every other row, and knot and cut off the ends to a length of 10 cm (4 in);

then, when you get up from the machine in a hurry, you won't take the whole lot with you!
4 Always wear comfortable clothes that will not get caught in the carriage, and tie back long hair.
5 Never be tempted to skimp on the time spent working out your tension square.
6 If you can, join a local knitting machine club, where there will always be someone who can help you with any problems.

MAKING IT SIMPLE
Although I have taken every care to ensure that the patterns in the book are as clear and straightforward as possible, there are a few extra details that I have included here which will augment the basic instructions provided.
PUNCHING CARDS: With a felt-tip pen, mark the needle arrangement on your punchcard using the illustrated card guide provided with each pattern. Double check that you have marked it correctly before punching it. The cards shown are for most makes of machine, but Toyota make some machines that knit in reverse. The easiest way to get round this is to punch the *card* in reverse, rather than to try and read the whole pattern in reverse, which could be rather muddling.

If a pattern requires a long punchcard, you can buy unmarked rolls that can be marked up to the length you need. When you have punched the card, mark the rows up the side with a pen, to correspond to the printed card designed for your machine. This is better than joining two punchcards together, because the overlapping numbered rows can be confusing and you will have to re-mark the second card so that the rows follow on in sequence. If only one colour is shown in one of the feeders during a pattern sequence, remove the second colour. Find out from your manual how to reset your needles, should you make a mistake or want to insert a second card.
WAXING: All yarns should be waxed by running them over the wax bobbin in the yarn feed, although most coned machine-ready yarns will probably be waxed ready to knit up. It is essential that all DK cotton yarn is waxed. Even so, some of the newer standard gauge machines may have difficulty with the yarn, so buy one ball

to try out before you commit yourself to a large quantity.

RIBBING: I have only used the ribbing attachment for the usual ribs. There are no racking patterns, jacquard rib, tubular knits or patterns using two beds, so a single bed (either standard or chunky) machine can work all the patterns. If you do not have a ribber you can work the ribs by hand as follows.

Ignore the welt instructions and cast on the required amount of stitches with waste yarn. Knit a few rows. Continue as pattern. Work the welt by hand by casting on with a rib needle the amount of stitches given in the pattern, using a pair of knitting needles of a suitable size for the yarn being used, and working it to the required length. Slip the first row of knitting, discarding the waste yarn onto a knitting needle, and holding both sets of stitches together, cast off onto a needle two sizes larger than the needles used for the welt. In my view this works far better than mock rib or reformed stitches. In many cases you cannot knit the welt by hand first and transfer the stitches to the machine, as you will find that the welt cast on edge will prevent the work being stretched far enough to be placed on to the needles.

Of course welts were originally knitted on to garments to make a hard-wearing and warm edge, but on today's fashionable garments (and with central heating), they are not always necessary, so if you do not have a ribber, then you can work a stocking stitch welt. After knitting the body of the garment, reduce the stitches on the first row, discarding any waste yarn, and place them on the machine. With four-ply and double-knitting yarns, reduce the stitches by about 30, and with chunky yarn, by about 20, and knit downwards, casting off the last row loosely. This edge will curl but you can press a natural fibre flat quite easily.

Always count the needles required for ribs from the right, and once you have hooked the stitches on to the main bed, increase one stitch on the left to centre your work.

CASTING OFF: Because I know that everyone has a different method of casting off, I have left the choice up to you in the patterns. However, latching off gives a good edge, and is much quicker. If the main tension dial has been up to number 8, then you can knit the last row at

tension dial 10. Using the latch tool, latch off (see diagram). If the main tension dial has been at 10, then you can still latch off by cheating slightly, and running the yarn through the carriage by hand, pulling down on the work as you go across to get as loose a row as possible. Obviously if your tension is set at a low level, set it at about four whole numbers higher and knit across the last row at this tension (eg. if your TD is 2, change it to TD 6). Most of the chunky tensions in these patterns are about 1–5, so allow the recommended four whole tensions higher, which should be loose enough. When latching off rib, knit the last row at a loose tension while the work is still hooked up to the ribber. Then either hook the stitches up to the main bed and latch off, or latch off up and down between the ribber and the main bed.

CARRIAGE: Knitting machine manufacturers used to give different starting sides for the carriage. These days it usually starts on the right. However, in case you have an older machine, or you have inherited one recently, I have tried to be flexible about carriage starting sides, so that you can continue to use the method with which you are happy. Only a few patterns stipulate carriage sides. Therefore the knitter may find in a

Latching off
1 Slip the stitch off the needle on to the latch tool, behind the latch.

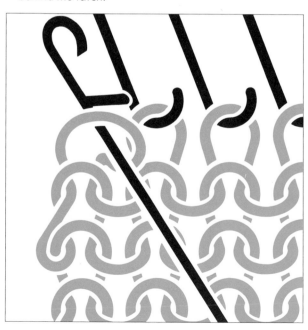

few cases that an extra row is needed in order for the carriage to be the correct side for the neck or shoulder shaping.

MAKING UP: If you can get used to joining up the shoulder seams and joining the sleeves to the body of the garment on your knitting machine, then you will be able to achieve a really professional finish. Always put in the ends down the side of the work, if you haven't already knitted them in. I prefer to knot them first, being careful not to distort the stitches. I often join the whole garment on the machine, using it like a linker. With a plain sweater in one colour, I may also join the sleeve and side seams on the right side which produces a decorative ridge on the shoulders, the top of the sleeves and the side and sleeve seams.

When I am unable to join up the whole garment on the knitting machine, I generally prefer to sew up garments on the sewing machine, but my new electric machine doesn't like sewing knitteds, so I have to resort to my ancient Singer, and using a straight stitch I sew as close to the edge as possible. All ribs I sew by hand and chunky sweaters have to be sewn by hand, after you have joined up as much as possible on your knitting machine.

SHAPING SHOULDERS: All the garments in the book have had their shoulders shaped and joined on the machine. Although the method involved requires a little practice, it is well worth learning because it is quick and gives a more professional finish.

Many knitters will still want to cast off and sew up their knitting by hand, so the instructions in the patterns are written with this in mind. But this is how to convert those instructions if you want to join up on the machine:
If the pattern reads:

> **B**ACK
> *SHAPE SHOULDERS:* Cast off 6(7:8) sts beg next 6 rows, 7 (8:9) sts beg next 2 rows and 8(8:9) sts beg next 2 rows. Cast off rem 28 sts.

this is how it will convert for shaping and joining on the machine:

> **B**ACK
> *SHAPE SHOULDERS:* * On opp side to carr, push 5(6:7) sts to HP. Set carr for partial knitting. K 1 row, push 1 more st to HP, adjacent to those already in HP *. Rep from * to

2 Slip the second stitch off the needle on to the latch tool, in front of the latch. Pull the second stitch through the first stitch.

3 Continue along the row to the last stitch. Loop the yarn in front of the latch, and pull through cut yarn.

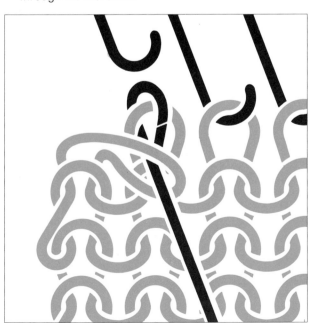

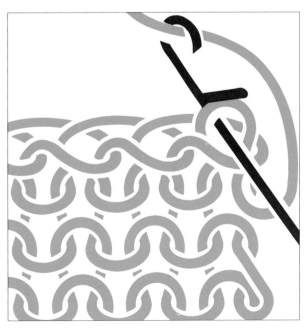

* 5 more times. ** On opp side to carr push 6(7:7) sts to HP, K 1 row, push one more st to HP **. Rep from ** to ** once. *** On opp side to carr push 7(7:8) sts to HP, K 1 row. Push one more st to HP as before ***. Rep from *** to *** once. **** On opp side to carr, push all sts in HP to WP, K 1 row ****. Rep from **** to ****. All sts now in WP. K several rows with WY and remove from machine.

If the pattern says:

FRONT
SHAPE SHOULDERS: Cast off 6(7:8) sts beg next row and next 2 alt rows, K 1 row, then cast off 7(8:8) sts beg next row and 8(8:9) sts on foll alt row.

To convert it:

FRONT
SHAPE SHOULDERS: K 1 more row than pattern, so that carr is at centre. * On opp side to carr push 5(6:7) sts to HP. Set carr for partial knitting. K 1 row, push 1 more st to HP, K 1 row *. Rep from * to * twice. On opp side to carr push 6(7:7) sts to HP, K 1 row, push 1 more st to HP, K 1 row. Push all sts in HP to WP. K 1 row across all sts.

If you are knitting a garment in a single colour:

Leave the front shoulder sts on the machine: with the R/S of back shoulder facing, place these sts on top of front sts, discarding WY only over these sts. K 1 row at TD 10. Latch off.

If you are knitting a two colour garment:

When shoulder sts have been pushed back to WP, K 1 row, then several rows with WY. Take work off the machine and replace it with the R/S facing. Place back shoulder sts on top with the W/S facing. K 1 row at TD 10. Latch off. Repeat on the other side. If you are attaching the neckband on the machine, join the second shoulder seam afterwards.

SHAPING ROUND NECKS: So that knitters can shape round necked garments as they wish, the patterns have been written for casting off. However, a much better edge is achieved if the stitches are held and either transferred on to a length of waste yarn and removed from the machine, or (if you wish to attach neckbands or collars by hand) knit one row and latch off. This produces an even edge, instead of fluctuating 'steps'. If the pattern instructions provided read:

Push centre 14 sts to HP and all rem sts on opp side to carr. Set carr for partial knitting. K 1 row, putting yarn under the first st in HP. K 2 rows. * Cast off 4 sts beg next row, K 1 row *. Rep from * to * twice more.

then convert them in this way:

Work as above until the instruction K 2 rows, and instead, K 1 row. (Carr at opp side to neck). * Push 3 sts to HP at neck edge, K 1 row, push 1 more st to HP, adjacent to those already in HP, and K 1 row *. Rep from * to * twice more. When all neck shaping on each side is completed, K several rows with WY over all the sts in HP in the centre of the neck and remove from machine, or K 1 row and latch off.

REFORMING STITCHES
By turning a stitch, you are able to make a knit stitch on the purl side of the fabric, or a purl stitch on the knit side of the fabric. Drop the stitch off the needle, with a latch tool re-knit (see diagram) and replace on the needle. You can do this with every stitch, along the row to make a garter ridge, or with the same stitch dropped down several rows, to form a vertical embossed knit stitch on the purl side of the fabric, as in aran patterns or for ribs.

JOINING UP ON THE MACHINE
1   If you have made a garment in a single colour, you can join up the sleeves to the body speedily on the machine, and, by so doing, give them a decorative edge. While the sleeve is still on the machine, take the joined back and front, and with the right

Reforming a stitch
1 Slip one stitch off the needle and drop down one row.

2 Insert latch tool, from the front, through the stitch and reknit.

3 Place the stitch on the empty needle.

Reforming a row of stitches
Repeat with every stitch along the row.

side facing, place the shoulder seam over the centre two stitches and the positioning markers on the front and back pieces, on each of the end stitches. Knit one row at tension dial 10, and latch off. If you have a chunky machine, you may have to push the needles right out in order to knit across. If your machine still refuses to knit, then knit this row by hand and latch off.

If you have knitted a two or more colour

garment, when the sleeve has been completed, knit several rows with waste yarn and remove your work from the machine. Leave the empty needles in working position, take the back and front, with the right side facing, pick up a loop from the row-ends between the positioning markers and place on the empty needles. Replace the sleeve on the machine with the wrong side facing. Knit one row at tension dial 10 and latch off.

2 If you want to join the neckband to the body of a garment on the machine, then first join one shoulder seam. When you have hooked the neckband up on to the main bed, take the front and back, and with the wrong side facing, place the stitches evenly from around the neckline on to the neckband stitches, picking up loops from the straight edges of neckline. Knit one row at tension dial 10, and latch off.

3 Collars are joined in the same way as the neckband, but *both* shoulder seams must be joined first. When you have hooked the collar up to the main bed, take the front and back pieces, and with the wrong side facing and starting at centre front, place as many stitches as you can on to the collar, before the work becomes too stretched. Cast these stitches off by hand, then place a few more stitches on to the collar and cast off. Continue in this way all round the neckline. Before you begin you will have to decide how many stitches and loops you will need to pick up, so that you can align the neck edge of your work evenly with the collar stitches.

4 When adding button bands to a collar, sew them on to the front opening of the garment. Join the collar as described above, but place half of the button band stitches on to the collar stitches at each end.

5 When adding button bands to a neckband sew them on to the front opening of the garment. With the wrong side facing, place the stitches from the button band on to the neckband and as many more stitches from around the neckline before the work becomes too stretched. Cast off these stitches by hand, place a few more stitches on to the neckband, and cast off. Continue

around the neckline, ending with all the stitches from the second button band.

6 In most cases the armbands of a garment have to be cast off and sewn on by hand, if they are to sit well and remain loose (see 'Cannes' 38-41). This is because the front and back of a garment cannot be stretched out to the width necessary for the knitter to be able to pick up loops from the row ends and place them on to the armband stitches in order to cast off both sets together. Always sew the *cast off edge* of the armband on to the front and back edges of the garment.

7 To ensure that the cuffs are always neat and close-fitting, many patterns advise that they should be attached on to the sleeve after it has been knitted. If experienced knitters want to knit the cuffs first then that is perfectly all right, as long as they feel sure that they can stretch the last row out to make the required amount of stitches for the first row of the pattern. If you have knitted a cuff first, space out the stitches carefully and place one loop on the empty needle from the adjacent stitch, and from the row below, to prevent any holes forming.

SHORT ROW WORKING

To me this is the most interesting aspect of machine knitting. Even with the most basic machine, without a punchcard, you can create the most wonderful designs. Short row working means pushing some stitches into holding position, every row or alternate row, in order to knit the remaining stitches in working position and create a triangular wedge, or decorative ridges and bobbles within the body of the knitting.

There are several designs in the book that involve this technique. They can all be done quickly and easily on the most basic machines so don't be put off by their intricate appearance!

1 'Entrelac' knitted in Argyll Finesse mohair (p114), takes a fraction of the time needed to knit an entrelac sweater by hand, even though you have the labour of transferring the stitches.

2 'Snuggler', in Sirdar Nocturne (p50), is

knitted in strips that are quickly joined up to make the cardigan.

3 'Champagne' (p110), in three of Pingouin's luxury yarns, is made by casting on at one side of the neck and working by short row all the way round to the opposite neck edge. This sweater is probably the quickest to make in the whole book, and it is very easy.

4 The 'Isosceles' sweaters (p22) are rather more complicated than the first three, especially if you just read the pattern, without knitting as you go! Try a sample piece using waste yarn and you will soon see the logic of the pattern and be able to manage the sweater.

Short row working can also be combined with a punchcard pattern:

1 'Gypsy Rose', in Sirdar Nocturne (p18), combines short row working on the two outer panels and knitting with a punchcard to make the flower motifs. The beads are all knitted into the sweater on the machine, slipped on to the relevant stitch as you are knitting.

2 The centre wedge of 'Parisienne', knitted in Rowan Soft Cotton (p82), is formed with short row working.

Normally when pushing stitches into holding position, for shaping necks and shoulders, you move a group on the opposite side to the carriage to holding position, set the carriage for partial knitting, and knit one row. Then you place the yarn lying over the top of the group of stitches in holding position under the first needle adjacent to the stitches in working position, knit one row and repeat. I prefer the method I have described below, which is quicker and gives a better finish, because you knit one more row on the stitch that would normally have the yarn slipped under it.

If the pattern specifies moving 10 stitches into holding position, push only 9 stitches to holding position, and knit one row. Then push one more stitch to holding position adjacent to those in working position and knit another row. The yarn will then be over the top of the last stitch, just as if you had slipped it over, and you will have the full complement of stitches.

The object of slipping the yarn over the last needle is to prevent a hole appearing in your work. With this method, you knit one more row across that stitch and the yarn is over the top, so your work will be doubly firm at this point. If you are working a dirndl skirt, for instance, in which there are several groups of stitches to be held, you will find that this method is much speedier.

BUTTONHOLES

Because an odd number of stitches is always required when knitting rib, a two stitch buttonhole on a buttonhole band can never be exactly in the centre. When I have specified that the buttonhole should be formed in the middle of a buttonhole band, as I have in most of the 'buttoning' patterns, you can make it so that it falls roughly across the middle stitches. The reason I have not suggested making a three stitch buttonhole, is that such a hole would be too large and look clumsy.

TENSION

Although machine manuals always provide sufficient information about tension squares, I feel that the importance of knitting at the correct tension cannot be emphasized too strongly. Some knitters I have employed in the past have been so eager to get through a garment, that they have just crossed their fingers and prayed that if they stick to the tension specified in the pattern, everything will work out well. This was largely due to the fact that they were unsure how to measure their tension swatches correctly, so I gave them this simple example which shows what happens to a piece of work if it is knitted at the wrong tension.

On a chunky machine:

> If the pattern states 20 sts and 26 rows = 10 cm (4 in), and the amount of sts is 110 and rows 104, then this piece of knitting should measure 56.5 cm (22 in) in width and 41 cm (16 in) in length. If you have 18 sts instead of 20, then your work will measure 62 cm (24 ½ in), making a difference of 13 cm (5 in) around the whole garment.

On a standard gauge machine:

> 8 sts to 2.5 cm (1 in) over 200 sts

MACHINE SELECTION GUIDE

	STANDARD	CHUNKY	STANDARD PUNCHCARD	CHUNKY PUNCHCARD
GYPSY ROSE				●
ISOSCELES		●		
BARNSTORMER		●		
SNAP			●	
RANGER			●	
CANNES	●			
ANGLER	●			
HARVEST	●			
SNUGGLER		●		
SHIPMATE		●		
TOKYO		●		
MISTRAL			●	
MONO			●	
FLOATING			●	
RAMBLER		●		
LEXICON			●	
PARISIENNE			●	
AERO	●			
TWISTER		●		
PERENNIAL			●	
PIXIE				●
SLALOM				●
SNOWFLAKES				●
CHAMPAGNE		●		
ENTRELAC		●		
GREY FLANNEL	●			
CHECKMATE			●	
EXECUTIVE			●	
VICE VERSA				●
CREEPY CRAWLIES			●	
EARL GREY			●	

will give a width of 63.5 cm (25 in), but if you only get 7 sts to 2.5 cm (1 in), then the width will be 72.5 cm (28 ½ in).

HELPFUL HINTS: With every garment you make it is wise to keep a notebook in which you can keep a record of the type and amount of yarn used, and the tension dial setting. If you knit the same pattern in the same yarn, but use a different colour, you will still have to re-do the tension swatch, because different colours affect the thickness of a yarn to a surprising degree.

As an additional help when you are knitting tension squares, sticky labels with the tension number written on them will remind you of what the tension was in certain areas of the sample square. You may be convinced that you won't forget the tension as you knit, but if you leave your work for a few days, you may well find that you cannot remember it.

If the tension in the pattern states 30 sts - 10 cm (4 in), push out 30 needles, leaving the adjacent needles at each side in non-working position. Push out a further 5 needles at each side. Cast on with waste yarn and knit a few rows. Change to the main colour, turn the tension dial to one number lower than the recommended tension number, and knit the amount of rows given for 10 cm (4 in). Stick a label marked with the tension dial number onto the work. Knit 2 rows with waste yarn, then turn the tension dial to the recommended tension and knit with the main colour the same rows as before. Stick on another marked label. Knit 2 rows with waste yarn, then turn the tension dial up to one number higher than the recommended tension and knit with the main colour the same rows as before. Stick on a marked label. Knit 2 rows with waste yarn and take the work off the machine.

If you are knitting a patterned swatch, then press it according to the instructions on the ball band, being careful not to distort the knitting. If it is a chunky swatch, then a gentle tug downwards before allowing the work to settle will help to give the knitting shape. Leave all swatches for a few hours, or overnight if possible to settle. Measure them carefully and select the tension (using your labels as guides) that matches the recommended one most exactly. If your square is almost there, then discipline yourself to try again,

setting your tension dial between the whole numbers.

PHOTOGRAPHS
The size of each garment photographed is given with each pattern, so that you can judge how a particular size looks on our size 10 (8) models. The male model has a 96.5-101.5 cm (38-40 in) chest, and the little girl model is six-and-a-half-years-old.

CARE OF GARMENTS
Taking care to follow the instructions on the ball bands when pressing garments is crucial. I have twice changed the whole structure of yarns that looked like wool but weren't by careless pressing. I didn't bother to read the manufacturers recommendations because I was so certain that it was wool and pressed the seams under a damp cloth. The imprint of the iron remained clearly up the side seam for all to see; it never disappeared! Since then, I have always taken care to keep the ball bands and follow the care instructions to the letter.

This is also very important when it comes to washing. When washing by hand, you must be careful not to lift a garment out of the water unsupported, because the weight of the water will stretch it. When you have rinsed it thoroughly, spin it in the spin cycle of your washing machine or spin dryer; never tumble dry. Ease it into shape when it is still damp and dry it flat away from direct sunlight. When it has dried, press it as you did when you first completed the knitting.

The reference (see note**) that appears throughout the patterns is to draw your attention to these preliminary guidance notes.**

GYPSY ROSE

Traditional floral motifs and beading bring touches of romance to this beautiful design.

GYPSY ROSE

MACHINE
Chunky 24 st punchcard.

MATERIALS
Sirdar Nocturne. 50 gm balls.
E 4(4:5) balls No: 574
F 3(4:4) balls No: 559
D 3 balls No: 564
C 4 balls No: 530
Crochet hook, fine enough to be inserted through wooden beads. 60 Yellow, 60 Green, 40 Red and 20 Blue wooden beads. Teazel Brush.

TENSION
Main Tension Dial approx No: 3
20 sts and 24 rows – 10 cm (4 in) square, measured over pattern.

MEASUREMENTS
To fit bust:
81–86.5(91.5–96.5:101.5–106.5) cm
32–34(36–38:40–42) in
Actual size:
96.5(106.5:117) cm
38(42:46) in
Length:
62(66:68.5) cm
24½(26:27) in
Sleeve length:
38 cm
15 in

ABBREVIATIONS
(see page 7)

NOTES
Photographed garment knitted to third size.
NB: Knit side is right side.
Punch cards illustrated before starting to knit.

BACK
Lock card 1 on row 1.
NB: Back worked in three vertical panels, after knitting welt.
Push 93(103:111) ndls to WP. Set machine for K1 P1 rib. With E, cast on selvedge. TD MT -3 RC 000. Rib 40 rows. Hook up to main bed, inc 1 st on L on all sizes and 2 sts on R on third size to centre work.
First Panel: Leaving 34(38:42) sts

nearest carr in WP, remove rem sts from machine on WY. Set carr for partial knitting. Break off E, replace with C. * RC 000. K 1 row, push the first st on opp side to carr to HP, K 1 row, push second st nearest carr to HP, K 1 row. Cont pushing one more st to HP every row to RC 34(38:42)*. Push rem st to HP, take carr across. RC 35(39:43). Break off C, replace with E. K 2 rows across all sts.
** With crochet hook, inserted through a red bead, take off the 5th st opp carr on to crochet hook, pull through bead and replace on ndl. Leave 3 sts then rep with a green bead, leave 3 sts and rep with a yellow bead. Cont in this sequence leaving 5 sts at near end**. With E, K 1 row, pushing down beads to enable carr to knit. Break off E. Push all sts to HP, except the first 2 sts nearest carr. RC 000. With D, K 2 rows, push 2 more sts (next to those in WP) from HP to WP. K 2 rows. Cont in this way pushing 2 more sts to WP every 2 rows, throughout, working to RC 8(10:12). Cont with shaping, K 4 rows F, 4 rows D, rep last 8 rows once, then K 4 rows F, K 6(8:10) rows D. RC 34(38:42). Replace carr on opp side. Work from * to * in foll colour sequence: K 7(9:11) rows C, 4 rows F, 4 rows C, rep last 8 rows once, then K 4 rows F, K 7 (9:11) rows C. Push rem st to HP, take carr across. RC 35(39:43). Break off C, replace with E. K 2 rows. Work from ** to **. With E, K 1 row. Break off E. Push all sts to HP, except the 2 sts nearest carr. With D, K 2 rows, push 2 more sts to WP, K 2 rows, cont in this way until all sts in WP. Slip sts on to WY and remove from machine.
Centre Panel: Return to the sts on welt, slip the next 26(28:30) sts on to the centre of the machine, inc 1 st each end of row. RC 000. With E, in feeder 1/A, K 1(3:5) rows, setting machine for patt on last row. With C in feeder 2/B, unlock card, K 6 rows. With E, K 1 row. With F in feeder 2/B, K 25 rows. Lock card. With E, K 1(3:5) rows. RC 34(38:42). With F, K 7(7:8) rows, with E, K 7(8:8) rows, with F, K 6(8:8) rows, with E, K

7(8:8) rows, with F, K 7(7:8) rows, with E, K 6(8:8) rows, RC 74(84:90) dec 1 st each end of last row. Slip sts on to WY and remove from machine.
Third Panel: Replace the rem 34(38:42) sts on to machine, over the same ndls as before. Set carr for partial knitting. Starting with carr on opp side, work from * as first panel, leaving sts on machine at RC 74(84:90).
YOKE: Place all sts on WY on to machine in correct order. Discard WY. Lock card 1 on row 1. With C, K 2 rows. Leaving the first 2(3:4) sts place next st through a yellow bead and on to machine as described for back, leave 3 sts and place a green bead on next st, leave 3 sts and place a blue bead on next st. Cont in this sequence, leaving 3(4:5) sts at opp end. K 1 row. Change to F in feeder 1/A, K 1 row, setting machine for patt. Unlock card and with E in feeder 2/B, K 6 rows. K 1 row with F. With C in feeder 2/B, K 25 rows. Lock card. With F, K 8 rows. With WY, mark the centre 44(46:48) sts. K a few rows with WY across all sts and remove from machine.

FRONT
First Panel: Pocket Lining: Push 34(38:42) ndls to WP. With E, cast on with 'e' wrap method. TD MT -1 RC 000. K 40 rows. Cont as first panel of back from * to end.
Third Panel: Pocket Lining: Push 34(38:42) ndls to WP. With E, cast on with 'e' wrap method. TD MT -1 RC 000. K 40 rows. Cont as third panel of back from * to end, slip sts on to WY and remove from machine.

WELT
Push 93(103:111) ndls to WP. Set machine for K1 P1 rib. With E, cast on selvedge. TD MT -3 RC 000. Rib 40 rows. Cast off the first 34(38:40) sts on R, and with a spare piece of E, cast off 33(37:41) sts on L, leaving 26(28:30) sts in centre, inc 1 st each end of row.
Centre Panel: Work as centre panel on back from RC 000 to end.
YOKE: Work as yoke on back to

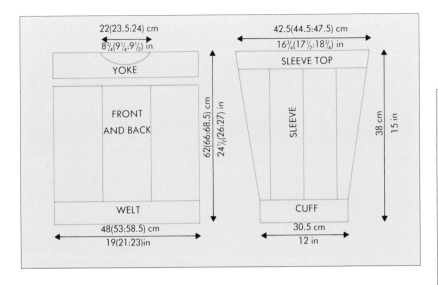

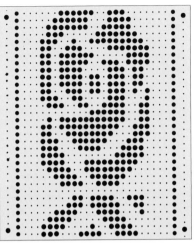

CARD 1

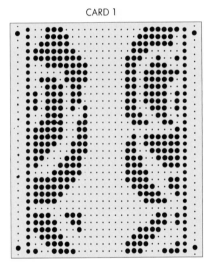

CARD 2

lock card.

SHAPE NECK: Push centre 38(40:42) sts and all rem sts on opp side to carr to HP. Set carr for partial knitting. K 1 row, putting yarn under first st in HP. K 2 rows. [Push 1 st nearest carr to HP, K 2 rows] 3 times. Carr at neck edge. With R/S of back shoulder sts facing, place on top of sts in WP. Cast off both sets of sts together. Leave the centre 38(40:42) sts in HP and the 3 sts from first side of neck shaping, push rem sts to WP. K 1 row putting yarn under the first st in HP, K 2 rows. Work as given for first side.

Neckband: Push the 44(46:48) sts in HP to WP. TD MT RC 000. With F, K 10 rows. Cast off. Back Neckband: With W/S of work facing, place the sts on WY at centre back neck, on to machine and work to match front neckband. Discard all WY.

Slip sts on to WY and remove from machine.

Gusset: Place the 6 sts on WY on machine. TD MT RC 000. With D, shape outer edge as follows: Inc 1 st at end of row 6(6:8), then inc 1 st on this edge every foll 6th (5th:4th) row to RC 67. 17(19:21) sts. Slip sts on to WY and remove from machine. Place rem 5 sts on WY on to machine. Inc 1 st at outer edge, then work as given for first side. Place the three groups of sts on the machine in the correct order. RC 67. 82(86:90) sts. With E, K 2 rows. Leaving the first 4 sts place a yellow bead on the next st, leave 3 sts place a green bead on next st, leave 3 sts place a red bead on next st. Cont to end of row, 5 sts rem. With E, K 1 row. Cont to inc as set to 84(88:94) sts, and AT THE SAME TIME work as follows: K 4 rows F and 4 rows E. RC 78. Cast off.

SLEEVES
Lock card 2 on row 1.
Push 59 ndls to WP. Set machine for K 1 P 1 rib. With C, cast on selvedge. TD MT -3 RC 000. Rib 20 rows. Hook up to main bed. On WY, take off the first 6 sts on R, and the first 5 sts on L. TD MT RC 000.

Centre panel: *** With C in feeder 1/A, K 1 row, setting machine for patt, inc 1 st each end of row. With D in feeder 2/B, unlock card, and K 6 rows. With C, K 1 row, with F in feeder 2/B, K 25 rows ***. Turn card back to row 1 and work from *** to ***, omitting inc on first row. Lock card. With C, K 1 row dec 1 st each end of row. RC 67.

MAKING UP
Sew centre panel on to the first and third panels, very neatly, on front, back and on to the gussets on sleeves. Sew pocket linings. Sew sleeves on to front and back to their full depth. Sew side and sleeve seams. Brush all over with a teazel brush without scratching the beads. Do not press, but keep one ball band for washing instructions.

DESIGNER TIP
On the third size when working centre panel, on some rows, end needles will select contrast colour. Before knitting, these needles must be pushed back to knit in main colour.

ISOSCELES

A dynamic duo in warm winter tones enhanced by
dramatic, colourful triangles in chenille.

ISOSCELES

MACHINE
Chunky.

MATERIALS
Rowan Yarns:
MAN'S, Aran 100 gm hanks.
Chenille 50 gm balls.
WOMAN'S, Aran 100 gm hanks.
Spun Tweed 100 gm hanks.
   MAN'S, Aran:
MC 800(800:900:900) gm No: 82
E   Chenille 1 ball No: 383
F   1 ball No: 384
D   1 ball No: 388
   WOMAN'S, Aran:
MC 800(800:900:900) gm No: 62
E   Spun Tweed 100 gm No: 758
F   100 gm No: 757
D   100 gm No: 754

TENSION
Main Tension Dial approx No: 5
16 sts and 24 rows – 10 cm (4 in)
square, measured over st.st.

MEASUREMENTS
To fit bust/chest:
   91.5–96.5(101.5–106.5:112–
   117:122–127) cm
   36–38(40–42:44–46:48–50) in
Actual size:
   106.5(117:127:137) cm
   42(46:50:54) in
Length:
   63.5(65:66:67.5) cm
   25(25½:26:26½) in
Sleeve length:
   43 cm
   17 in

ABBREVIATIONS
(see page 7)

NOTES
Photographed garments knitted to
second and fourth sizes.
NB: Knit side is right side.
Chenille is used double.

BACK
NB: Mark each end of row
62(66:62:66).
On R of centre, push the first ndl to
WP, then push 42(46:50:55) ndls
each side to WP. Set machine for
K1 P1 rib. With MC, cast on
selvedge. TD MT -3 RC 000. Rib 24
rows. Hook up to main bed. TD MT
RC 000. K 6(6:8:10) rows. Carr R.
   ** First Motif: Push all sts to L of
centre to HP. Set carr for partial
knitting, K 1 row. Push first st on R
of centre to HP. K 2 rows. [Push
next st to HP (next to those already
in HP), K 2 rows] 5 times. Push one
more st to HP, K 1 row. Carr R.
Break off yarn. RC 20(20:22:24).
Take RC out of working. Push all sts
on R to HP, replace carr on L. Push
all sts to L of centre to WP. K 1 row,
put yarn under first st in HP. K 2
rows. [Push one more st to HP (next
to those already in HP) K 2 rows] 5
times, then push one more st to HP,
K 1 row. Carr L. Break off yarn.
Push all sts to HP. Replace carr on
R. Push the first st on R of centre to
WP. Slot E between second and
third ndls on R, take it over all sts in
HP, and place in carr. * Slip small
claw weight onto centre st. K 2
rows. [Push first st in HP on L to WP,
K 1 row, push one more st on R in
HP, to WP, K 1 row] 6 times *. Carr
R. Break off yarn, push all sts to
WP. Reset RC. With MC K 6 rows.
RC 26(26:28:30).
   Second and Third Motifs: On R
of centre, push st Nos:1 – 24 and
all sts on L to HP, K 1 row [Push 1 st
to HP (next to those already
in HP), K 2 rows] 6 times. Push one
more st to HP, K 1 row.
Carr R. Break off yarn. RC
40(40:42:44). Take RC out of
working. Push all sts on R of centre
to HP. Replace carr on L. Keeping
st Nos: 1 – 23 on L of centre and all
sts on R of centre in HP, push rem
sts to WP. K 1 row. [Push 1 st to HP
(next to those already in HP) K 2
rows] 6 times. Push one more st to
HP. K 1 row. Break off yarn, push
sts in WP to HP. Push st Nos: 1 – 24
on R of centre and 1 – 23 on L of
centre to WP. Carr L. Slip yarn
between ndl Nos: 24 and 25, over
all sts in HP, and into carr. K 1 row.
Put yarn under first st in HP on R. [K
1 row, push 1 st on L to HP, (next to

those already in HP), K 1 row, push
1 st on R to HP (next to those
already in HP)] 6 times. K 1 row.
Break off yarn. Push all sts to HP.
Replace carr on R.
   Second Motif: On L of
centre push st No: 24 to WP.
With D, slot yarn between ndl
Nos: 22 and 23 on L and over sts in
HP as before. Work from * to *,
changing to F when 8 rows worked.
Break off D and F. Push these 13
sts to HP.
   Third Motif: Push st No: 25
on R of centre to WP. Slot F
between ndl Nos: 26 and 27, over
sts in HP as before. Work from * to
* in 2 rows F and 2 rows E. Break
off E and F. Reset RC. Push all sts to
WP **. With MC, K 6 rows to RC
46(46:48:50). Rep from ** to **
using D instead of E for first motif
and working 2 rows E and 2 rows D
on second motif and on third motif
working 8 rows F and 6 rows D. RC
80(80:82:84). K 6 rows. Rep from
** to ** using F instead of E for first
motif and working 8 rows E and 6
rows F on second motif and 2 rows
D and 2 rows E on third motif. RC
120(120:122:124). K to RC
122(126:128:132).
   SHAPE SHOULDERS: (see note).
Cast off 7(8:9:10) sts beg next 2
rows, 8(8:9:10) sts beg next 2 rows
and 8(9:10:11) sts beg next 4 rows.
Cast off rem 23(25:25:27) sts.

FRONT
Work as back to RC 66(66:68:70).
Carr R.
   SHAPE NECK: Transfer centre st
to adjacent ndl on R. Slip all rem sts
on L onto WY and remove from
machine. Push empty ndls to NWP.
At neck edge dec 1 st on 4th and
every foll 4th row until 11(12:
12:13) sts dec and AT THE SAME
TIME, cont in patt. When first rep
completed, work to RC 106(106:
108:110) and work third motif.
Cont straight to RC 123(127:129:
133).
   SHAPE SHOULDER: Cast off
7(8:9:10) sts beg next row,
8(8:9:10) sts beg next alt row,
8(9:10:11) sts on foll alt row. K1
row. Cast off rem 8(9:10:11) sts. K1
row. Replace sts on WY on to
machine over the same ndls as

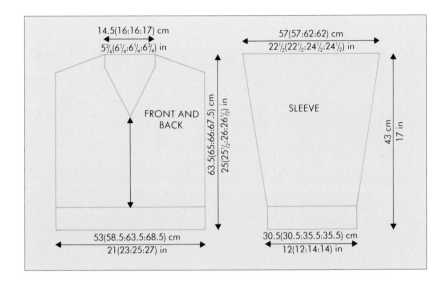

before. Carr R. Shape neck and
cont in patt to match back.

SLEEVES
Push 43(43:49:49) ndls to WP. Set
machine for K1 P1 rib. With MC,
cast on selvedge. TD MT -3 RC 000.
Rib 12 rows. Hook up to main bed.
Push 2(2:3:3) empty ndls on R to
WP and 3(3:4:4) empty ndls on L to
WP at each side. Transfer end sts
evenly over these ndls, picking up a
loop from the adjacent st one row
below and placing it on the empty
ndl. 48(48:56:56) sts. TD MT
RC 000. Shape sides by inc 1 st
each end of 3rd and every 3rd row
7 times in all, then on 4th and
every 4th row 7 times, then on 5th
and every 5th row 7 times and AT
THE SAME TIME work as follows: K
10 rows, then work from ** on back
to RC 90. 90(90:98:98) sts (see
note) Cast off.

COLLAR
(2 pieces alike)
Push 35 ndls to WP. Set machine
for K1 P1 rib. With MC, cast on
selvedge. TD MT -3 RC 000. Rib
168(172:176:180) rows. Cast off.

MAKING UP
If you have joined shoulders and
sleeves on machine, sew sleeve and
side seams. Sew one side of collar
from base of vee to centre back
neck. Rep on the other side. Join
centre back seam. Overlap at the
front, and sew down on outside
and inside. If you are sewing
garment by hand, then join
shoulders with a flat seam. Sew in
sleeves to the markers, then
complete as above. Press with a
damp cloth. Hand wash only in
soap flakes 30°C. Short spin, ease
to shape, dry flat away from direct
sunlight.

**DESIGNER TIP:
Knitting a sample
swatch of this pattern
will help you to get to
grips with this unusual
technique.**

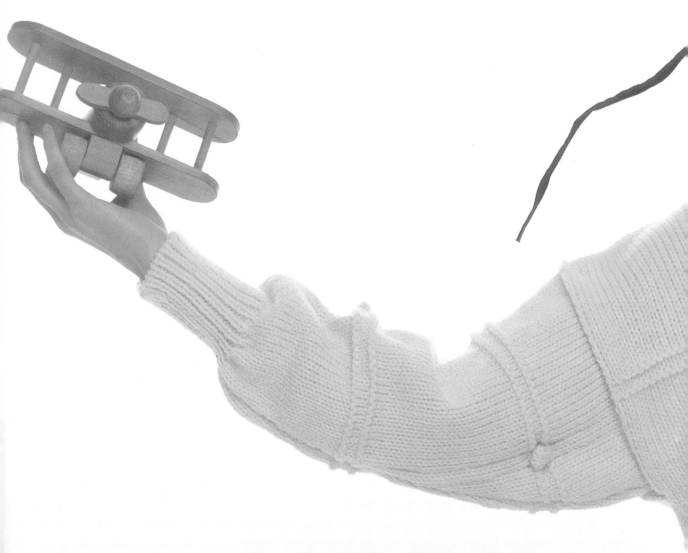

BARN**STORMER**

An out-sized show-stopping chunky knit that will keep you up on a thermal all day long.

BARN**STORMER**

MACHINE
Chunky.

MATERIALS
Phildar Shoot. 50 gm balls.
   14(15:17) balls No: 30.
   One wooden toggle.

TENSION
Main Tension Dial approx No: 5
17 sts and 25 rows – 10 cm (4in)
square, measured over st.st.

MEASUREMENTS
To fit bust:
   86.5-91.5(96.5-101.5:106.5-
   112) cm
   34-36(38-40:42-44) in
Actual size:
   101.5(112:122) cm
   40(44:48) in
Length:
   63.5(65:66) cm
   25(25$\frac{1}{2}$:26) in
Sleeve length:
   46 cm
   18 in

ABBREVIATIONS
(see page 7)

NOTES
Photographed garment knitted to
second size.
NB: Knit side is right side.

BOBBLES
With WY cast on 2 sts. * K 6 rows.
Change to MC. K1 row, inc 1 st
each end of next row, K 4 rows.
Dec 1 st each end of next row. K 1
row. (RC 8). Cut off MC. Change to
WY and work from * 25 times in all.
Cut through the WY rows.

BACK
NB: Mark each end of rows
74(78:82) with WY.
Push 85(95:105) ndls to WP. Set
machine for K1 P1 rib. Cast on
selvedge. TD MT -3 RC 000. Rib 24
rows. Hook up to main bed, inc 1 st
on L to centre work. TD MT RC 000.
K 29 rows. On R of centre take st
No: 30 off ndl and drop down 29
rows, reknitting with latch tool to
form a P st on R/S of fabric.
Replace on empty ndl. Rep with st
Nos: 27 and 2. Rep on L of centre
with the same sts.
   ** K 1 row. On R of centre
take the first st off ndl, drop
down one row and reknit with
latch tool. Replace on the empty
ndl. Rep with every st. K 2 rows.
With a 2 prong tool, slip st Nos: 28
and 29 on R of centre onto tool,
take a bobble, with W/S facing,
place the first row on to the empty
ndls, discarding WY. Place the last
row on top. Push bobble between
work and machine, replacing the 2
sts on tool on top. Push into E
position to aid knitting. Rep over st
Nos: 28 and 29 on L of centre and
st Nos: 1 and 1 in centre. K 2 rows.

On R of centre take the first st off
ndl, drop down one row and reknit
with latch tool. Replace on the
empty needle. Rep with every st **.
K to RC 67. On R of centre take st
No: 30 off ndl and drop down 33
rows, reknit as before and place on
empty ndl. Rep with st Nos: 27 and
2. Rep with same sts on L. Work
from ** to **. K to RC 105. On R of
centre take st No: 30 off ndl and
drop down 33 rows, reknit as
before and place on empty ndl.
Rep with st Nos: 27 and 2. Rep with
same sts on L. Now work from ** to
**. Cont to RC 134(138:142).
   SHAPE SHOULDERS: (see note).
NB: Just before casting off each
group, drop down and reknit the
same sts as before. Cast off 8(9:10)
sts beg next 8 rows. Cast off the
rem 22(24:26) sts.

FRONT
Work as back to RC 84(88:92).
   SHAPE NECK: Drop down st Nos:
2 and 2 in centre, as before and
reknit. Place the centre 22(24:26)
ndls and all rem sts on opp side to
carr on to WY and remove from
machine. On first side, work
straight to match back to RC
134(138:142).
   SHAPE SHOULDER: Cast off
8(9:10) sts beg next row and foll alt
rows 3 times in all. K 1 row, cast off
rem 8(9:10) sts. Replace sts on WY
on to machine over the same ndls
as before. Reset RC. Carr centre.
Cast off the first 22(24:26) sts, then
cont over the rem 32(36:40) sts to
match the first side.

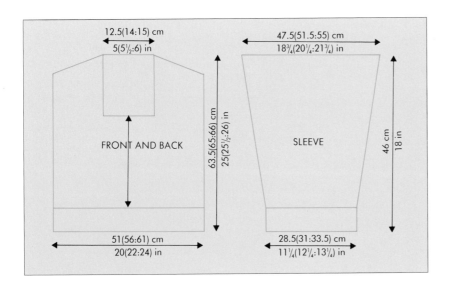

12.5(14:15) cm
5(5½:6) in

47.5(51.5:55) cm
18¾(20¼:21¾) in

63.5(65.5:66) cm
25(25½:26) in

FRONT AND BACK

SLEEVE

46 cm
18 in

51(56:61) cm
20(22:24) in

28.5(31:33.5) cm
11¼(12¼:13¼) in

SLEEVES
Push 41(45:47) ndls to WP. Set machine for K1 P1 rib. Cast on selvedge. TD MT -4 RC 000. Rib 24 rows, hook up to main bed. Spread the end 3 sts over 6 ndls, so there are 3 empty ndls in between. Take a loop from the adjacent st, from one row below, and place loop on empty ndl. 47(51:55) sts. Inc 1 more st on L. TD MT RC 000. Work in pattern as back, (omitting bobbles on the second and third sizes over st Nos: 27 and 30 each side on row 32) and shaping sides by inc 1 st each end of 13th(8th :3rd) row, then every foll 5th row to RC 92. 80(86:92) sts (see note).
    Cast off.

COLLAR
(2 pieces alike)
Push 91(93:93) ndls to WP. Set machine for K1 P1 rib. Cast on selvedge. TD MT -3 RC 000. Rib 39(41:43) rows. Cast off.

MAKING UP
If you have joined shoulders and sleeves on to front and back on the machine, then sew sleeve and side seams. If sewing garment by hand, sew shoulder seams with a flat seam. Sew in sleeves to markers. Sew sleeve and side seams. Sew cast off edge of collar from centre back neck down front. Rep on the other side. Overlap right side over left side and sew on to cast off sts. Sew on a toggle as shown in photograph. Press according to instructions on the ball band and keep one ball band for washing instructions.

DESIGNER TIP:
Remember to reverse the back seam of the collar so that it is disguised.

SNAP

**A star for the evening.
Flash dash in bronze and
silver lurex on black.**

SNAP

MACHINE
Standard Gauge 24 st punchcard.

MATERIALS
Twilleys Goldfingering. 25 gm balls.
MC 9(11:13) balls No: 31
D   4(4:5) balls No: 35
E   3(3:4) balls No: 9

TENSION
Main Tension Dial approx No: 9
30 sts and 40 rows – 10 cm (4 in)
square, measured over pattern.

MEASUREMENTS
To fit bust:
   81(86.5:91.5) cm
   32(34:36) in
Actual size:
   91.5(96.5:101.5) cm
   36(38:40) in
Length:
   56(58.5:61) cm
   22(23:24) in

ABBREVIATIONS
(see page 7)

NOTES
Punch card illustrated before
starting to knit.
Photographed garment knitted to
second size.
NB: Knit side is right side.

BACK
The plain bands are worked first,
then joined on the machine to the
patterned bands. First Band: Push
200 ndls to WP. With E, cast on
with 'e' wrap method. TD MT RC
000. K 8 rows. Change to MC, K
32(36:42) rows. Change to E, K 8
rows. Cast off. Work second and
third bands as first band.

WELT
Lock card on row 1.
Push 129(139:149) ndls to WP. Set
machine for K1 P1 rib. With MC,
cast on selvedge. TD MT –2 RC
000. Rib 34 rows. Hook up to main
bed, inc 1 st on L to centre work. TD
MT RC 000. Join bands:
   * With D, K 2 rows, setting
machine for patt on last row.
With D in feeder 1/A and C in
feeder 2/B, unlock card. K 13 rows.
Lock card. With D, K 3 rows. K
several rows with WY and remove
from machine *.
   Push 130 (140:150) ndls to
WP. Take the first band and
** with R/S facing, pick up the loops
from the first row in MC, leaving
the 8 rows in E hanging down
in front **. Place the loops on the
ndls as follows: *** place one loop
on each of the first 15(20:25) ndls,
[then place 2 loops on each of the
next 2 ndls and 1 loop on next ndl]
(5 loops reduced to 3 sts) 20 times
in all, then place 1 st on each of the
last 15(20:25) ndls ***.
   With W/S of welt panel facing,
place the sts on WY on top of
band sts, discard WY and cast off
both sets of sts together. With
W/S of first band facing and with
the 8 rows of E hanging down
between work and machine, pick
up the last row in MC and work
from *** to ***. Lock card on row 1
and work from * to *. Take the
second band, work from ** to **,
then from *** to ***. With W/S of
patt panel facing, place the sts on
WY on top of band sts, discard WY.
Cast off both sets of sts together.
With W/S of second band facing
and with the 8 rows of E hanging
down between work and machine,
pick up the last row in MC and
work from *** to ***. Lock card on
row 1 and work from * to *. Take
the third band, work from ** to **,
then from *** to ***.
   With W/S of patt panel facing,
place the sts on WY on top of
band sts, discard WY. Cast off
both sets of sts together. With W/S
of third band facing and with the
8 rows of E hanging down
between work and machine, pick
up the last row in MC and work
from *** to ***. Lock card on row 1.
RC 000. With D, K 2 rows, setting

machine for patt on last row. With
D in feeder 1/A and C in feeder
2/B, unlock card. K in patt to RC
16. Card row No: 15.
   SHAPE NECK: (see note). Push
the centre 20(22:24) sts and all rem
sts on opp side to carr to HP. Set
carr for partial knitting. K 1 row.
Put yarn under the first st in HP. K 2
rows. Cast off the foll sts at beg of
next and every foll alt row: 6, 5, 4,
2, 1. Cont to RC 32. Lock card.
With D, K 1 row. K a few rows with
WY and remove from machine.
Replace the rem sts on WY on to
machine. Reset card and ndls (see
manual). Leaving the centre
20(22:24) sts in HP, replace rem sts
to WP. Work to match first side.
With a spare piece of D cast off the
centre sts.

FRONT
Work as back, leaving the sts from
the second shoulder on the
machine. Place the back shoulder
sts on top with R/S facing. With D,
cast off both sets of sts together.
Rep with rem shoulder sts.

NECKBAND
(2 pieces alike)
Push 73(75:83) ndls to WP. Set
machine for K1 P1 rib. With MC,
cast on selvedge. TD MT –2. Rib 12
rows (see note). Cast off.

ARMBAND
(2 pieces alike)
Push 159(163:173) ndls to WP.
Work as given for neckband.
   Cast off.

MAKING UP
Sew cast off edge of armbands
from centre of the second band on
back to centre of the second band
on front. Repeat on other side. Sew
side seams. Join edges of
neckband. Do not press but keep
one ball band for washing
instructions.

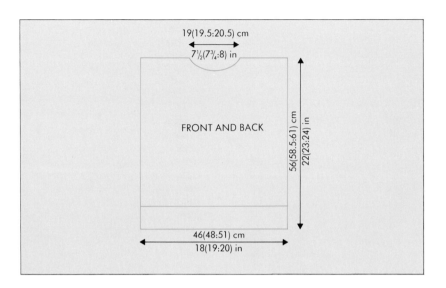

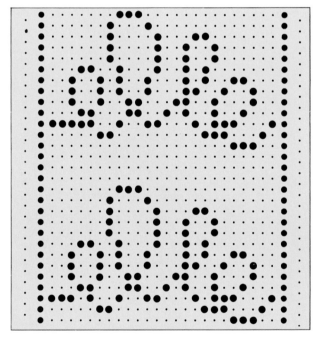

DESIGNER TIP:
This pattern is very easy, but because there are several repeats, you must keep careful notes of your progress so that you can find your place quickly when coming back to your work after an interruption.

RANGER

**Stunning colours combine to add
unconventional zest to a classic design.**

RANGER

MACHINE
Standard Gauge 24 st punchcard.

MATERIALS
Rowan Yarns Fine Nepp Yarn. 250 gm cones.
E   1(1:1:2) cone No: 62
F   1 cone No: 12
H   1 cone No: 90
G   1 cone No: 44
2 small buttons.

TENSION
Main Tension Dial approx No: 7
30 sts and 45 rows – 10 cm (4 in) square, measured over pattern.

MEASUREMENTS
To fit chest:
    96.5(101.5:106.5:112:117) cm
    38(40:42:44:46) in
Actual size:
    101.5(106.5:112:117:122) cm
    40(42:44:46:48) in
Length:
    65(66:66:67:68.5) cm
    25½(26:26:26½:27) in
Sleeve length:
    47(47:49.5:49.5:52) cm
    18½(18½:19½:19½:20½) in

ABBREVIATIONS
(see page 7)

NOTES
Photographed garment knitted to fifth size.
NB: Knit side is right side.
Punch card illustrated before starting to knit.

PATTERN
With the first colour in feeder 1/A and the second colour in feeder 2/B, K as follows: 2 rows E/-, 2 rows F/E, 2 rows F/-, 2 rows F/E, 2 rows F/G, 2 rows F/E, 2 rows F/-, 2 rows F/E, 2 rows E/-, 2 rows E/G, 2 rows E/-. Rep last 4 rows 6 times. RC 46 (Card row 47), 10 rows E/H, RC 56 (Card row 57). * 2 rows E/-, 2 rows F/E, 2 rows F/-, 6 rows F/G, 1 row H/-, 2 rows H/E, 1 row H/-, 6 rows F/G, 2 rows F/-, 2 rows F/E, 2 rows -/E, 2 rows H/E, 2 rows H/-, 6 rows H/F, 1 row G/-, 2 rows G/E, 1 row G/-, 6 rows H/F, 2 rows H/-, 2 rows H/E*.

BACK
Lock card on row 1.
NB: Mark each end of row 146 with WY.
Push 153(159:167:173:181) ndls to WP. Set machine for K1 P1 rib. With E, cast on selvedge. TD MT – 4 RC 000. Rib 36 rows. Hook up to main bed, inc 1 st on L to centre work. TD MT K 1 row, setting machine for patt. RC 000. Unlock card, K in patt to RC 108.
    ** Turn card back to row 57, (see manual for resetting ndls) and rep from * to * once **. Rep from ** to ** once.Turn card back to row 1, K in patt to RC 242(248:248:252:258). Lock card.
    SHAPE SHOULDERS: (see note). With E, cast off 9(10:10:10:11) sts beg next 2 rows, 9(10:10:11:11) sts beg next 4 rows, 10(10:11:11:12) sts beg next 6 rows. Cast off rem 40(40:42:44:44) sts.

FRONT
Work as back to RC 108. Turn card back to row 57. Remove the centre 8 sts and all rem sts on opp side to carr from machine on WY. K in patt as back on rem sts to RC 150.
    SHAPE NECK: Dec 1 st at neck edge on next and every foll 5th row 16(16:17:18:18) times in all. Cont straight to RC 242(248:248:252: 258). (Work one extra row for other side of neck.) Lock card. Carr at outer edge.
    SHAPE SHOULDER: Cast off 9(10:10:10:11) sts beg next row, 9(10:10:11:11) sts beg next alt row and foll alt row, K 1 row, then cast off 10(10:11:11:12) sts beg next row and foll alt row. K 1 row and cast off rem 10(10:11:11:12) sts. Replace sts on WY onto machine, over the same ndls as before. Reset card to row 57. Carr centre. RC 108. Cast off 8 sts beg first row, cont to match first side.

SLEEVES
Lock card on row 1.
Push 80(82:82:86:90) ndls to WP. TD MT. With WY, cast on and K a few rows. With E, K 1 row, setting machine for patt. RC 000. Unlock card, K in patt, shaping sides by inc 1 st each end of 6th(5th:6th: 6th:6th) rows 28(6:29:30:30) times and on second size cont on every 6th row 23 times and AT THE SAME TIME K to card row 37, cont to inc as set. Turn card on to row 47 and K to RC 98. Turn card back to row 57 and K to RC 150. Turn card back to row 1 and K to RC 176(176:180:180:188). 136(140:140:146:150) sts (see note). Cast off.

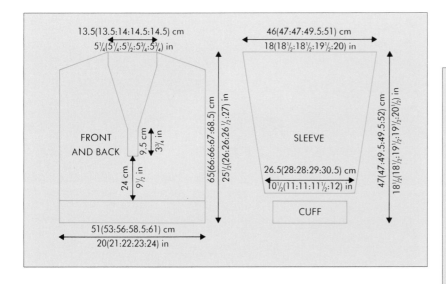

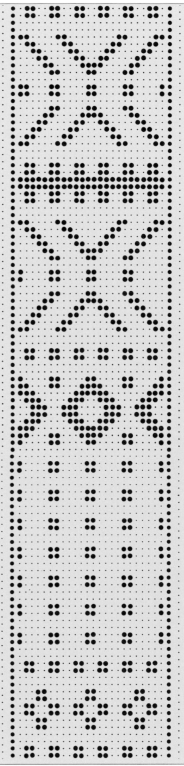

CUFFS
Push 59(61:61:63:67) ndls to WP.
Set machine for K1 P1 rib. With E,
cast on selvedge. TD MT -4 RC 000.
Rib 24 rows. Hook up to main bed,
inc 1 st on L on first and fourth
sizes. 60(61:61:64:67) sts. With
W/S of sleeve facing, place the first
row on to cuff sts as follows: [Place 2
sts on first ndl and 1 st on each of
the next 2 ndls] along row. K 1 row
loosely by hand. Cast off.

NECKBAND
(2 pieces alike)
Push 13 ndls to WP. Set machine
for K1 P1 rib. With E, cast on
selvedge. TD MT – 4 RC 000. Rib
162(170:170:178:184) rows.
   Cast off.

MAKING UP
If you have joined shoulder seams
and sleeves on to body on machine,
then sew on neckbands and sew
sleeve and side seams. Position
buttons as in photograph, sewing
through both bands. If sewing
garment by hand, join shoulder
seams with a flat seam, sew on
sleeves to front and back between
markers, sew sleeve and side
seams. Sew on neckbands and sew
on buttons through both bands.
Press all seams with a damp cloth,
then the whole garment. Hand
wash only in soap flakes, 30°C,
short spin, ease to shape, dry flat
away from direct sunlight.

DESIGNER TIP:
**The buttons are purely
decorative on this
garment, so instead of
having to make
buttonholes, you can
simply sew the button
through both bands.**

CANNES

Be something to write home about from the beach in this colourful holiday top.

CANNES

MACHINE
Standard Gauge.

MATERIALS
Rowan Yarns Mercerised Cotton.
250 gm cones.
C   2 cones No: 302
E   1 cone No: 320
D   1 cone No: 323
G   1 cone No: 322
F   1 cone No: 307
    8 safety pins.

TENSION
Main Tension Dial approx No: 7
30 sts and 40 rows – 10 cm (4 in)
square, measured over st.st.

MEASUREMENTS
To fit bust:
    86.5–91.5(96.5–101.5:106.5-
    112) cm
    34–36 (38–40:42–44) in
Actual size:
    96.5(106.5:117) cm
    38(42:46) in
Length:
    56 cm
    22 in

ABBREVIATIONS
(see page 7)

NOTES
Photographed garment knitted to
third size.
NB: Knit side is right side.

BACK
NB: Mark each end of row 104
with WY. Take RC out of working
when knitting strips.
Push 143(157:171) ndls to WP. Set
machine for K1 P1 rib. With C, cast
on selvedge. TD MT-4 RC 000. Rib
2 rows in each of the foll colours:
G, C, F, C, E, C, D, C, G, C. Hook
up to main bed, inc 1 st on L to
centre work. TD MT RC 000. With
C, K 10 rows, D, K 18 rows and C,
K 10 rows. K 2 rows in each of the
foll colours: G, C, F, C, E, C, D, C,
G. With C, K 9 rows. RC 65.
FIRST CROSS ROW: Keeping 9
sts to R of centre in WP,* push all
rem sts to HP. Set carr for partial
knitting. Slot C between the first
and second sts in HP next to those
in WP, take yarn over the sts and
into feeder. K 22 rows, pulling
slightly on work. Break yarn. Slip sts
on to a safety pin, dropping down
between work and machine. Push
empty ndls to NWP *. Push the 9 sts
to L of centre from HP to WP.
**With C, K 22 rows introducing
yarn for the first row as before. Slip
sts on to a safety pin dropping
down between work and machine.
Push empty ndls to NWP***. Slip the
loops from the last of the 9 C rows
on to empty ndls. Set carr for st.st.
With C, K 1 row. With E, K 18 rows.
Slip 9 sts to R of centre on to a pin
and remove from machine. Rep on
L. On R of centre, push up the strip
and place the sts on pin on to 9 ndls
on LEFT. Rep with strip knitted on L
of centre, placing on the 9 ndls on
RIGHT. Slip the sts from last C row
(on pins) on top of strips. With C, K
8 rows.

SECOND CROSS ROW: Keeping
st Nos: 21 – 29 on R of centre in
WP, work from * to *. Push st Nos:
12 – 20 on R of centre to WP
work from ** to ***. Work on
L of centre in the same way. Slip
loops from the last of the 8 C rows
on to the empty ndls. Set carr for
st.st. With C, K 1 row. K 2 rows in
each of the foll colours: G, C, F, C,
E, C, D, C, G. With C, K 1 row. Slip
sts from ndl Nos: 12 – 29 on R of
centre onto a pin, and remove from
machine. Pick up strips, crossing as
before, and replacing on the empty
ndls. Replace sts from the last C
row on top. Rep over st Nos: 12 –
29 on L. With C, K 8 rows.
THIRD CROSS ROW: Keeping st
Nos: 41 – 49 on R of centre in WP,
work from * to *. Push st Nos: 32 –
40 in R of centre into WP, work
from ** to ***. Work on L of centre
in the same way. Also work from
beg of first cross row to ***. Slip the
loops from the last C row on to the
empty ndls. Set carr for st.st. With
C, K 1 row, with G, K 18 rows, with
C, K 1 row. Slip st Nos: 32–49 on R
on to a pin. Rep on L. Slip centre 18
sts on to a pin. Pick up the strips,
crossing as before, and replace on
the empty ndls. Replace work on
top. With C, K 8 rows.
FOURTH CROSS ROW: Keeping
st Nos: 61–69 on R, in WP, work
from * to *. Push ndl Nos: 52– 60
on R to WP and work from ** to ***.
Work on L of centre in the same
way. Also work over st Nos: 12 –
29, as second cross row, on each
side. Slip loops from last C row on to
empty ndls. Set carr for st.st, with C,
K 1 row. K 2 rows in each of the foll
colours: G, C, F, C, E, C, D, C, G.
Slip st Nos: 52–69, and 12–29 on R
on to a pin. Rep on L. Cross strips as
before, placing on the empty ndls.
Replace work on top. With C, K 9
rows. RC 178.

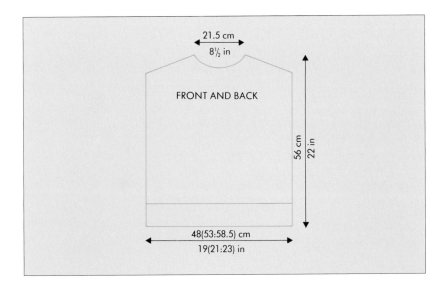

21.5 cm
8½ in

FRONT AND BACK

56 cm / 22 in

48(53:58.5) cm
19(21:23) in

SHAPE NECK: (see note). RC 000. Push centre 20 sts and all rem sts on opp side to carr to HP. Set carr for partial knitting. With F, K 1 row, slipping the yarn under the first st in HP. K 2 rows. Cast off 5 sts beg next and foll alt row. K 1 row, cast off 4 sts beg next row, 3 sts on next alt row, 2 sts on next alt row. K 1 row. Dec 1 st at neck edge on next and every alt row 3 times in all. (22 sts dec). K to RC 18. Change to C. K 4 rows.

SHAPE SHOULDERS: (see note). Cast off 8(9:10) sts beg next row and next 2 alt rows. K 1 row. Cast off 8(10:12) sts beg next and foll alt row. K 1 row. Cast off rem 8(10:12) sts. Leaving the centre 20 sts in HP, push rem sts to WP. Work to match first side.

FRONT
Work exactly as back.

NECKBAND
(2 pieces alike)
Push 85 ndls to WP. Set machine for K1 P1 rib. With C, cast on selvedge. TD MT –4 Rib 12 rows. Hook up to main bed (see note). Cast off.

ARMBAND
(2 pieces alike)
Push 159 ndls to WP. Set machine for K1 P1 rib. With C, cast on selvedge. TD MT –2 RC 000. Rib 40 rows. Cast off.

MAKING UP
If you have joined shoulders and neckband on the machine, sew up edges of neckband. If you are sewing garment by hand, then join shoulders with a flat seam, sew cast off edge of neckband around neck, sew edges of neckband. Sew cast off edge of armband on to front and back between the markers, sew under seam and side seams. Press with a damp cloth. Hand wash only in soap flakes, 30°C. Short spin, ease to shape, dry flat away from direct sunlight.

DESIGNER TIP:
It is a good idea to try out the technique of knitting in the crosses before you embark on the actual garment.

ANGLER

Layers of rippling colours sway across this sweater and catch everyone's attention.

ANGLER

MACHINE
Standard Gauge.

MATERIALS
Rowan Yarns 3 ply botany. 350 gm
cones. 1 cone each of
MC No: 61
D   No: 1
E   No: 12
F   No: 90
G   No: 17
H   No: 51
J   No: 621
    9 large safety pins.

TENSION
Main Tension Dial approx No: 5
32 sts and 48 rows – 10 cm (4 in)
square, measured over st.st.

MEASUREMENTS
To fit bust:
    86.5 – 96.5 (101.5 – 112) cm
    34–38(40–44) in
Actual size:
    101.5 (117) cm
    40(46) in
Length:
    58.5(61) cm
    23(24) in
Sleeve length:
    44.5(42) cm
    17½(16½) in

ABBREVIATIONS
(see page 7)

NOTES
Photographed garment knitted to
second size.
NB: Knit side is right side.

BACK
NB: Mark each end of row
220(220).
Push 161(183) ndls to WP. Set
machine for K1 P1 rib. With MC,
cast on selvedge. TD MT –3 RC
000. Rib 36 rows. Hook up to main
bed, inc 1 st on L to centre work. TD
MT RC 000. [With MC, K 2 rows,
with D, K 2 rows] 8 times. RC 32.
* Next row: Slip st Nos: 20/21, on R
of centre on to a safety pin. Push
empty ndls to NWP. Rep with st
Nos: 40/41, 60/61 and on 2nd
size: 80/81. Rep on L. On both
sizes, st No: 1 on R and No: 1 on L.
Push down pins, between work and
machine. With F, K 10 rows. Break
off F. Slip sts on pins on to the
empty ndls, with the floats in front.
With D, K 2 rows, with MC, K 2
rows, with D, K 2 rows, with MC, K
2 rows, with D, K 2 rows.
    With transfer tool take a loop
from the first D row (10 rows below)
under ndl No: 5 on L of centre and
place on st above. Rep with every st
through to st No: 16. Rep over st
Nos: 25 – 36, 45 – 56, 65 – 76 and
on 2nd size 85 – 92. Rep on R
making 8(9) small hems *. Rep from
* to * 4 times, using the foll colours
each time instead of F. 1st rep: Use
E. 2nd rep: Use G. 3rd rep: Use H.
4th rep: Use J. Rep from * to * 5
times working 2 rows in the foll
colours: F, E, G, H and J, instead of
10 rows with F. Rep from * to * 5
times using the foll colours each
time instead of F. 1st rep: Use J.
2nd rep: Use H. 3rd rep: Use G.
4th rep: Use E. 5th rep: Use F. Cont
in 2 row stripes as follows: With
MC, K 2 rows, with D, K 2 rows. Rep
last 4 rows to RC 354(364).
    SHAPE SHOULDERS: (see note).
With MC, cast off 9(10) sts beg next
4 rows, 9(11) sts beg next 6 rows,
10(11) sts beg next 2 rows. Cast off
rem 52(56) sts.

FRONT
Work as back to RC 340(350).
    SHAPE NECK: (see note). Push
centre 12(16) sts and all rem sts on
opp side to carr to HP. Keeping
stripes correct, set carr for partial
knitting and K 1 row. Put yarn
under first st in HP. K 2 rows. Cast
off the foll sts beg next and every
foll alt row: 7, 6, 4, 2 and 1. Cont
to RC 354(364).
    SHAPE SHOULDER: With MC,
cast off 9(10) sts beg next row and
foll alt row. K 1 row. Cast off 9(11)
sts beg next row and foll 2 alt rows.
K 1 row. Cast off rem 10(11) sts.
Leaving the centre 12(16) sts in HP,
push all rem sts to WP. Work as for
first side. With a spare piece of
yarn, cast off the centre 12(16) sts.

SLEEVES
Push 79(85) ndls to WP. Set
machine for K1 P1 rib. With MC,
cast on selvedge. TD MT –3 RC
000. Rib 36 rows. Hook up to main
bed, inc 1 st on L to centre work. TD
MT RC 000. Shape Sides by inc 1 st
each end of every 8th(6th) row 20
times in all, then every 7th row, and
AT THE SAME TIME work in patt as
follows: [With MC, K 2 rows, with D,
K 2 rows] 10(8) times. RC 40(32).
Work as back from * to * omitting st
Nos: 60/61 and 80/81 and
making hems over st Nos: 25–36
and 45–56 on R and L and centre
12. Rep from * to * 8 times more,
with the foll colours instead of F. 1st
rep: Use E. 2nd rep: Use G. 3rd
rep: Use H. 4th rep: Use J. 5th rep:
Use H. 6th rep: Use G. 7th rep: Use
E. 8th rep: Use F, working
increased sts into patt. With MC, K
2 rows, with D, K 2 rows. Rep last 4
rows 8(7) times more. Cont to RC
256(244) and 142(160) sts (see
note). Cast off.

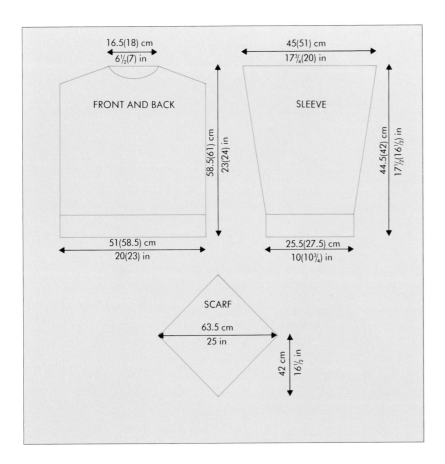

NECKBAND
Push 125(133) ndls to WP. Set machine for K1 P1 rib. With MC, cast on selvedge. TD MT -2. Rib 4 rows. (See note). Cast off.

SCARF
With MC, cast on 2 sts with 'e' wrap method. TD MT RC 000. With MC, K 2 rows, with D, K 2 rows. Rep last 4 rows and AT THE SAME TIME inc 1 st each end of every alt row to 200 sts. With MC, dec 1 st each end of every alt row to 2 sts. Cast off.

MAKING UP
If you have joined shoulder seams, neckband and sleeves on the machine continue as follows: Sew sleeve and side seams. Fold scarf in half lengthwise. Sew edges together. Sew straight edge on to the inside of neckband, leaving 10 cm (4 in) open at the front. If sewing garment by hand, join shoulders with a flat seam. Sew in sleeves to the markers, then complete as above. Press seams with a damp cloth. Hand wash only in soap flakes, 30°C. Short spin, ease to shape, dry flat away from direct sunlight.

DESIGNER TIP:
On the scarf, mark each end of every 20th row with WY, to make sewing up easier and even.

HARVEST

Creamy cotton scattered with harvesting motifs brings a breath of country air to your wardrobe.

HARVEST

MACHINE
Standard Gauge.

MATERIALS
Hayfield Raw Cotton. 50 gm balls.
    Sweater: 15(16:17:18) balls.
    No: 001.
    Skirt: 12(13) balls No: 001.
    Elastic for skirt band.

TENSION
Main Tension Dial approx No: 10
26 sts and 36 rows – 10 cm (4 in)
square, measured over st.st.

MEASUREMENTS
SWEATER:
To fit bust:
    91.5(96.5:101.5:106.5) cm
    36(38:40:42) in
Actual size:
    101.5(106.5:112:117) cm
    40(42:44:46) in
Length:
    62 cm
    24½ in
Sleeve length:
    46 cm
    18 in
SKIRT:
To fit hips:
    96.5(101.5) cm
    38(40) in
Actual size:
    101.5(106.5) cm
    40(42) in
Length:
    76 cm
    30 in

ABBREVIATIONS
(see page 7)

NOTES
Photographed garments knitted to
fourth size on sweater and second
size on skirt.
NB: Purl side is right side.

SWEATER

TWISTS
Push 8 ndls to WP. With WY, cast
on, K a few rows. TD MT * RC 000.
With MC, K 14 rows. Cut off MC
leaving a 10 cm (4 in) length. With

WY, K 10 rows, cut off WY *. Rep
from * to * 39 more times. Cut
through the centre of the WY rows,
to make 40 strips.

LEAVES
Push 4 ndls to WP. With 'e' wrap
method, cast on with MC. TD MT K
1 row. Set carr for cord knitting (i.e.
carr knits only in one direction). K 9
rows (5 rows knitted). Reset carr for
st.st. K 2 rows. Inc 1 st each end of
next row. K 1 row. [Inc 1 st each
end of next row and transfer st 2
on to 3 on R of centre. Rep on L. K 2
rows] 3 times.
    Next row: Only transfer sts as set.
K 2 rows. [Dec 1 st each end of row,
transfer sts as before, K 2 rows] 3
times. [Dec 1 st each end of next
row. K 1 row] twice. 26 rows. RC 32.
Slip rem sts on to WY and remove
from machine. Make 15 more
leaves.
    Knit into work as follows: With
W/S facing flatten stem and place
2 sts from cast on edge on to ndls 45
and 46. K 2 rows. [Pick up one side
of edge sts and place on the same
2 ndls. K 2 rows] 3 times. Leaf now
starts to inc, so take one side of
edge st, place on ndl 44, rep on ndl
47. K 2 rows.
    Next row: Place on to ndls 41 and
50, K 2 rows.
    Next row: Place on to ndls 40 and
51, K 2 rows. Leaf now starts to dec
so knit in, in reverse, over 10, 8, 6
and 4 sts, with 2 rows in between
each time. Slip rem sts off WY and
on to ndl Nos: 45 and 46. Cont
placing rem leaves as given in patt.

CORDS
Push 3 ndls to WP. With 'e' wrap
method, cast on with MC. Set carr
for cord knitting (i.e. carr knits in
one direction only). TD MT RC 000.
** K 450 rows. Cast off. Make 15
more. Cast on and work to **. K
230 rows. Cast off. Make 3 more.
Cast on and work to **. K 330
rows. Cast off. Make 3 more.

BACK
NB: Mark each end of row
118(114:110:106).
Push 133(139:145:151) ndls to

WP. Set machine for K1 P1 rib.
Cast on selvedge. TD MT -1 RC
000. Rib 30 rows. Hook up to main
bed, inc 1 st on L to centre work. TD
MT RC 000.
    Work patt as follows: K 2 rows.
Row 3: On R of centre, transfer
st No: 2, on to st No: 3 and st No:
60 on to st No: 61. Rep on L.
K 4 rows. Cont in this way,
transferring sts and working 4 rows
throughout and AT THE SAME
TIME work as follows: Row 7: On
ndl No: 45 and 46 on R of centre
introduce a leaf. Rep on L. On ndl
Nos: 7 – 14 on R of centre
introduce a twist: with W/S of twist
facing, place 8 sts on to these ndls,
discarding WY. Let twist drop. Rep
on L. Cont to RC 19, knitting in leaf
as given and making eyelets as
given. Row 20: *** Take a twist and
keeping it dropped down, turn it
twice clockwise and with R/S facing
discard WY, slipping the sts on to
the same ndls as before. Rep on
L ***.
    Take another twist and with W/S
facing place on ndls Nos: 18 - 25
on R. Let it drop. Rep on L. Cont
to knit in leaf, K to RC 32. Row 33:
Rep row 20 from *** to ***. (Leaf
completed.) K to RC 36. On R of
centre drop st No: 30 off ndl and
down to row 1. Latch up to make a
P st, replace on ndl. Rep on L. K 2
rows. Row 39: On R of centre,
transfer the foll sts: 2 on to 3, 5 on
to 6, 10 on to 11, 15 on to 16, 20
on to 21, 25 on to 26, 30 on to 31,
35 on to 36, 40 on to 41, 45 on to
46, 50 on to 51, 55 on to 56 and
60 on to 61. Rep on L. K to RC 46.
Row 47: As row 39. K to RC 50.
Hook a piece of WY over ndl No:
30 on R and L. K to RC 53. Row 54:
On ndl Nos: 47 - 54 on R of
centre, hook in a twist. Rep on L.
Hook a leaf on to ndl Nos: 15 and
16 on R of centre. Rep on L. K 13
rows knitting in leaf. RC 66. Row
67: Turn twists as before and
place on to sts. Hook
a twist over ndl Nos: 36-43 on R of
centre. Rep on L. Cont knitting in
leaves. K 13 rows. RC 79. Row 80:
Turn twists as before and place
on to sts. (Leaf completed). K to RC
84. Drop st No: 30 on R of centre
off ndl and down to the WY
marker. Latch up as a P st and
place on to ndl. Rep on L. K 2 rows.
Rep rows 39 to 47. K to RC 98.
Mark ndl No: 30 with WY on R and
L. K to RC 101. Rep from row 7 -
36 placing second twist on row 114
and twisting on row 127. (Leaf

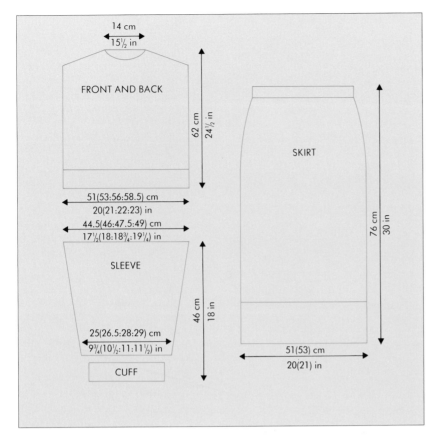

14 cm
15½ in

FRONT AND BACK

62 cm
24½ in

51(53:56:58.5) cm
20(21:22:23) in

44.5(46:47.5:49) cm
17½(18:18¾:19¼) in

SLEEVE

46 cm
18 in

25(26.5:28:29) cm
9¾(10½:11:11½) in

CUFF

SKIRT

76 cm
30 in

51(53) cm
20(21) in

SKIRT

BACK
Push 163(175) ndls to WP. Set machine for K1 P1 rib. Cast on selvedge. TD MT RC 000. Rib 100 rows. K a few rows with WY and remove from machine. Place these sts on main bed as follows: Push 134(146) ndls to WP, place 1 st on each of the first 2 ndls, then [place 2 sts on next ndl and 1 st on each of the next 4 ndls] to last 3 ndls, place 1 st on each of the last 3 ndls. TD MT RC 000. K 4 rows, dec 1 st each end of next and foll 15th rows 8 times in all. 118(130) sts. K 9 rows, dec 1 st each end of next and every foll 7th row 7 times in all. 104(116) sts. RC 162. On R of centre drop down st No: 30 to top of rib and latch up as a P st. Replace on ndl. Rep on L. Set machine for K1 P1 rib, transfer sts, dec 1 st on L. Put in comb and hang on weights. TD MT RC 000. Rib 24 rows. Hook up to main bed. Place first row of rib onto ndls to make a hem. Cast off. Work front as back.

MAKING UP
SKIRT: Sew up side seams, thread elastic through and sew up hem. *SWEATER:* Join shoulders and sleeves on machine or by hand. Sew cast off edge of collar evenly on to neckline. Sew sleeve and side seams. Cords: Using a 450 row cord. Starting at outer edge, pull cord through top eyelet, take it diagonally over to next bottom eyelet, push through to back of work, then through eyelet directly above, cont in this way to the centre, leaving the vertical eyelets without cords. Turn the cord and slot through eyelets to make crosses. Fasten down. Rep with 450 row cords over front and back and tops of sleeves. Use a 330 row cord on the centre of each sleeve and a 230 row cord at bottom of sleeves. Press seams according to instructions on ball band. Keep one ball band for washing instructions.

DESIGNER TIP:
All ribs are improved by slipping a knitting needle into the selvedge row and pulling away from the body of the rib, but this is crucial when knitting in cotton.

completed.) K 1 more row. RC 132. Drop down st No: 30 to marker and reknit as a P st. Rep on L. K 2 rows. Rep rows 39 to 47. K to RC 146. Mark st Nos: 10, 20, 30, 40 and 50 on R of centre with WY. Rep on L. K to RC 170. On R of centre drop down st No: 10 to the WY marker and latch up as a P st. Place on ndl. Rep with st Nos: 20, 30, 40 and 50. Rep on L. Cont transferring st Nos: 2 and 60 on R and L every 4 rows as set. K to RC 188.
    SHAPE SHOULDERS: (see note). Cast off 9(10:11:11) sts beg next 2 rows, 10(10:11:11) sts beg next 2 rows, 10(10:11:12) sts beg next 2 rows and 10(11:11:12) sts beg next 4 rows. Cast off rem 36 sts.

FRONT
Work as back to RC 174.
    SHAPE NECK: (see note). Push centre 10 sts and all rem sts on opp side to carr to HP. Set carr for partial knitting. K 1 row, slipping yarn under the first st in HP. K 2 rows. Cast off 5 sts beg next row, K 1 row. Cast off 4 sts beg next row, K 1 row, cast off 2 sts beg next and foll alt row. K 4 rows.
    SHAPE SHOULDER: (see note). Cast off 9(10:11:11) sts beg next row and the foll sts on every alt row: 10(10:11:11), 10(10:11:12) and 10(11:11:12) sts. K 1 row, cast off rem 10(11:11:12) sts. Reset RC

to 174. Keeping the centre 10 sts in HP, push all rem sts to WP. Carr at outer edge. Work as for first side. With a spare length of MC, cast off the centre 10 sts.

SLEEVES
Push 64(68:72:76) ndls to WP. With WY, cast on, K a few rows. Change to MC. TD MT RC 000. Work in patt as back omitting edge eyelets and only work the centre eyelets and the centre two panels and AT THE SAME TIME, inc 1 st each end of row 22 and every foll 5th row. Work rows 39–47 over all sts. Cont to RC 146. 114(118:122:126) sts (see note). Cast off.

CUFFS
Push 53(57:59:59) ndls to WP. Set machine for K1 P1 rib. Cast on selvedge. TD MT -1 RC 000. Rib 26 rows, hook up to main bed. With K/S of work facing, place the first row of sleeve on to cuff sts, reducing sleeve sts evenly across row. K 1 row loosely, by hand. Cast off.

COLLAR
Push 111 ndls to WP. Set machine for K1 P1 rib. Cast on selvedge. TD MT RC 000. Rib 30 rows, hook up to main bed (see note). Cast off.

SNUGGLER

Elegance and practicality unite in this luxurious mohair cardigan.

SNUGGLER

MACHINE
Chunky.

MATERIALS
Sirdar Nocturne. 50 gm balls.
C   6(7) balls No: 552
D   3(3) balls No: 574
E   4(5) balls No: 519
10 buttons
Teazel brush.

TENSION
Main Tension Dial approx No: 3
16 sts and 28 rows – 10 cm (4 in)
square, measured over st.st.

MEASUREMENTS
To fit bust:
    86.5–101.5(101.5–117) cm
    34–40(40–46) in
Actual size:
    117(127) cm
    46(50) in
Length:
    74 cm
    29 in

ABBREVIATIONS
(see page 7)

NOTES
Photographed garment knitted to
first size.
NB: Knit side is right side.

PATTERN
(Worked in 4 horizontal strips,
joined on the machine).

LEFT FRONT SLEEVE AND
LEFT FRONT
FIRST STRIP: Push 30 ndls to WP.
TD MT, with WY, cast on and K a
few rows. Carr L. Change to E,
placing a marker on the first st on
R. With E, K 4 rows, with C, K 2
rows, with E, K 6 rows. Set carr for
partial knitting. RC 000.
    * With D, K 1 row, push the first
st on L to HP. K 1 row. Push the
second st on L to HP, K 1 row. Cont
to push one more st to HP, every
row, marking st on R on row 22. K
to RC 30. Push the rem st in WP
to HP. Break off D.

Carr L. Take RC out of working *.
** With C, push the first 2 sts on L to
WP, K 2 rows, change to E push
next 2 sts to WP, K 2 rows **. Rep
from ** to ** until all sts in WP.
*** Reset RC to 000. K in stripes as
follows: 12 rows D, 4 rows E, 2 rows
C, 6 rows E, 12 rows D, 4 rows E, 2
rows C, 6 rows E ***. [Work from *
to * without marking row 22, then
from ** to **, using only E
throughout] twice. On second size
only, with C, K 6 rows ****.
    SHAPE NECK: Carr L. With C,
cast off 5 sts beg next row, K 1 row,
cast off 2 sts beg next and foll alt
rows 4 times in all. K 2 rows.
Cast off.
    SECOND STRIP: RC 000. With E,
cast on 2 sts with 'e' wrap method.
Place marker on the first st on L.
Carr L. K 2 rows. Work in stripes of
2 rows C and 2 rows E and AT THE
SAME TIME inc 1 st on R on next
and every foll alt row to RC 58. (30
sts) Carr L. With C, work as first strip
from * to * then from ** to ** using
only E. Reset RC. With C, work as
first strip from * to *, then from ** to
** using only E. RC 118. Carr L. On
second size only, K 2 rows C, 2
rows D and 2 rows C. Both sizes: K
2 rows D, 2 rows C, 2 rows D, 2
rows C, 2 rows D and 2 rows C ****.
Cast off.
    Join the two strips as follows:
Push 74(78) ndls to WP. With R/S of
first strip facing, and with marker at
top, place this st on first ndl, then
cont along strip, picking up loops
from the row-ends evenly on to ndls,
to cast off edge of strip. Take the
second strip and with W/S facing,
and marker at top, place a loop
from the marked st on to first ndl,
then cont along strip, picking up
loops as before, matching colours,
and ending at cast off edge. Cast
off both sets of loops together.
    THIRD STRIP: Push 30 ndls to
WP. Carr R. With 'e' wrap method
cast on with C. Place a marker on
first st on L. RC 000. ***** K 1 row.
Push first st on R to HP, K 1 row,
push second st on R to HP, K 1 row.
Cont in this way until all sts in HP.
Carr R. Take RC out of working.
With E, push the first 2 sts on R to
WP, K 2 rows. With D push the next
2 sts to WP, K 2 rows. Cont with 2
rows E and 2 rows D, until all sts in

WP. Carr R *****. Rep from ***** to
***** once. With E, K 12(18) rows
****. Cast off.
    Join second and third strips
as follows: Push 44 (48) ndls
to WP. With R/S of second strip
facing, pick up loops as before,
from the end of the increasing to
the cast off edge. With the W/S of
the third strip facing, with marker
at top, place loops from the row-
ends on top of second strip as
before, matching colours. Cast off.
    FOURTH STRIP: Push 30 ndls to
WP. With 'e' wrap method, cast on
with C. Place a marker on first st on
L. K in stripes as follows: 10 rows C,
2 rows E, 2 rows D, 2 rows, E, 2 rows
D, 2 rows E, 10 rows C, 4 rows E, 2
rows D, 4 rows E, 10 rows C, 4 rows
E, 2 rows D, 4 rows E, 12(18) rows
C ****. Cast off.
    Join third and fourth strips as
follows: Push 44(48) ndls to WP.
With R/S of third strip facing, pick
up loops as before. With W/S of
fourth strip facing, pick up loops
and place on top of third strip.
    Cast off.

RIGHT BACK SLEEVE AND
RIGHT BACK
Work all strips as left front sleeve
and left front with exceptions given
below: Work first strip to ****, do
not shape neck K straight with C
18(24) rows. K several rows with
WY and remove from machine.
Second strip: Work to ****. K 2 rows
D, 2 rows C and 2 rows D, K several
rows with WY and remove from
machine. Third strip: Work to ****,
with E, K 6 rows, K several rows
with WY and remove from
machine. Fourth strip: Work to ****,
with C, K 6 rows. K several rows
with WY and remove from
machine. Join all strips as left front
sleeve and left back, pushing
78(82) ndls to WP instead of
74(78).

RIGHT FRONT SLEEVE AND
RIGHT FRONT
Work as left front sleeve and left
front, reading R for L and L for R.

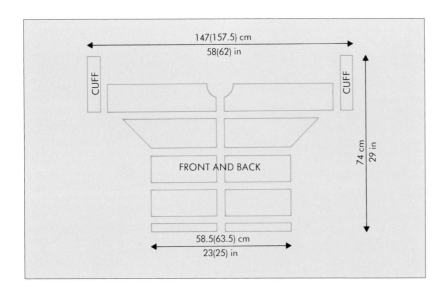

147(157.5) cm
58(62) in

CUFF

CUFF

FRONT AND BACK

74 cm
29 in

58.5(63.5) cm
23(25) in

LEFT BACK SLEEVE AND LEFT BACK

Work as right back sleeve and right back reading R for L and L for R.

Join left sleeve top seam as follows: Push 86(90) ndls to WP. With R/S of left front sleeve facing, place loops on ndls as before, from the first row to start of neck shaping. With W/S of left back sleeve facing, place loops on top of first sleeve, matching colours and stripes and omitting back neck sts. Cast off. Rep on right sleeve.

Join centre back seam as follows: First Strip: Push 30 ndls to WP. With R/S of left back facing, take the 30 sts on WY and slip on to ndls. With W/S of right back facing, place sts on WY on top of left back sts. Discard WY. Cast off both sets of sts together with C. Rep with next three strips, casting off in the correct colour.

CUFFS

Push 43 ndls to WP. Set machine for K1 P1 rib. With C, cast on selvedge. TD MT – 2 RC 000. Rib 16 rows. Hook up to main bed. With W/S of sleeve facing, place the sts on WY on to cuff sts as follows: [Place 2 sts on first ndl, 1 st on each of the next 2 ndls] to end of row. Cast off both sets of sts together.

BACK WELT

Push 91(99) ndls to WP. Work as rib on cuff. With W/S back facing, place a loop from the row-ends, evenly on to welt sts. Cast off both sets of sts together.

FRONT WELT

Push 43(47) ndls to WP. Work to match back welt.

BUTTON BAND

Push 11 ndls to WP. Set machine for K1 P1 rib. With C, cast on selvedge. TD MT –1 RC 000. Rib 130 rows. Cast off. Buttonhole band: Work as button band making a 2 st buttonhole (see note and manual) on the following rows: 5, 20, 35, 50, 65, 80, 95, 110 and 125. Cast off.

COLLAR

Push 101 ndls to WP on both beds. Set machine for K1 P1 rib. With C, cast on selvedge. TD MT–2 RC 000. Rib 6 rows. Make a 2 st buttonhole on R on next row, over st Nos: 5 and 6. Rib 30 rows, make a 2 st buttonhole on next row. Rib 6 rows. Cast off.

MAKING UP

Sew button bands on to fronts. Sew cast on edge of collar on to neckline and on to button bands. Fold inside, sew down cast off edge. Sew up front edges of collar. Sew sleeve and side seams. Sew on buttons. Brush all over with a teazel brush to release pile. Keep one ball band for washing instructions. Press according to the instructions on the ball band.

DESIGNER TIP: When joining two strips, use the correct colour for casting off.

SHIPMATE

**Ahoy there! Clear primary colours sail across the deep
blue of this smart cardigan.**

SHIPMATE

MACHINE
Chunky.

MATERIALS
Lister Machine Washable Aran.
40 gm balls.
MC 7(8:8) balls No: 461
G   1(2:2) balls No: 321
D   1 ball No: 2754
E   1 ball No: 3227
F   1 ball No: 3226
     4 buttons.

TENSION
Main Tension Dial approx No: 4
18 sts and 28 rows – 10 cm (4in)
square, measured over st.st.

MEASUREMENTS
To fit chest:
    66(71:76) cm
    26(28:30) in
Actual size:
    71(76:81) cm
    28(30:32) in
Length:
    40.5(46:48) cm
    16(18:19) in
Sleeve seam:
    33(35.5:38) cm
    13(14:15) in

ABBREVIATIONS
(see page 7)

NOTES
Photographed garment knitted to
second size.
NB: Purl side is right side.

TRIANGLES
Push 10 ndls to WP. With D, cast on
with 'e' wrap method. Hang a
small claw weight on to sts. TD MT
RC 000. K 2 rows. Dec 1 st each
end of next row and every foll alt
row until 2 sts remain. RC 10. Slip
sts on to WY. Remove from
machine. Make 17 more with D, 16
with E and 17 with F.

BACK
NB: Mark each end of row
70(74:78).
Push 65(69:75) ndls to WP. Set
machine for K1 P1 rib. With MC,
cast on selvedge. TD MT-3 RC 000.
Rib 10 rows. Hook up to main bed,
inc 1 st on L to centre work.
66(70:76) sts. TD MT RC 000. [With
MC, K 2 rows, with G, K 2 rows]
3(3:4) times. * K2 rows MC. RC
14(14:18).
    Introduce triangles as follows:
Take an 'F' triangle, with K/S facing
and 2 sts on WY uppermost, place
a loop from the end st of first row
on to st 5 on R of centre. Rep on L.
Let it drop. Take an 'E' triangle and
on R of centre, leave 2 sts from first
triangle, then place a loop from the
first row on to next st. Leave 8 sts
and place a loop from the other
end of first row on to next st. Rep
on L of centre with a 'D' triangle.
On R of centre, take a 'D' triangle,
leave 2 sts from last triangle and
place a loop from the end st on to
next st, leave 8 sts and place a
loop on to next st. Rep on L of
centre with an 'E' triangle. There
are 4(6:8) sts rem from end triangle
to edge of work on both sides. Push
triangles down so they don't catch
in carr. K 2 rows.

Centre Triangle: Place a loop
from each end of the 3rd row on to
ndl Nos: 4 and 4 each side of
centre. Rep with rem triangles. K 2
rows.
    Centre Triangle: Place a loop
from each end of the 5th row on to
ndl Nos: 3 and 3 each side of
centre. Rep with rem triangles. K 2
rows.
    Centre Triangle: Place loops as
before from the 7th row on to ndl
Nos: 2 and 2, rep with rem
triangles. K 2 rows.
    Centre Triangle: Place the sts on
WY on to ndls 1 and 1 each side of
centre, rep with rem triangles. K 4
rows. With G, K 2 rows. Rep from *
4 times as follows: First rep: Place
triangles as follows: reading R to L.
F, D, centre one E, F, D. Second
rep: E, F, centre one D, E, F. Third
rep: D, E, centre one F, D, E. Fourth
rep: F, D, centre one E, F, D. [With
MC, K 2 rows, with G, K 2 rows]
4(6:7) times. With MC, K 1 row. RC
109(117:125). K a few rows with
WY and remove from machine.

LEFT FRONT
Push 29(31:35) ndls to WP. Set
machine for K1 P1 rib. With MC,
cast on selvedge. TD MT -3 RC 000.
Rib 10 rows. Hook up to main bed
inc 1 st on L on first and second
sizes. TD MT RC 000. [With MC, K 2
rows, with G, K 2 rows] 3(3:4)
times. K 2 rows MC.
    Introduce triangles in the same
way as back. On R of work, leave
the first 3(5:8) sts, introduce a 'D'
triangle on to next st, leave 8 sts and
pick up loop on to next st. Leave 2
sts and introduce an 'E' triangle. 5
sts remain between last triangle and

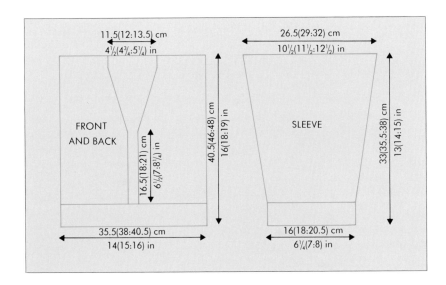

11.5(12:13.5) cm
4½(4¾:5¼) in

26.5(29:32) cm
10½(11½:12½) in

40.5(46:48) cm
16(18:19) in

33(35.5:38) cm
13(14:15) in

16.5(18:21) cm
6½(7:8¼) in

FRONT AND BACK

SLEEVE

35.5(38:40.5) cm
14(15:16) in

16(18:20.5) cm
6¼(7:8) in

left side of work. Cont to RC 46(50:58) knitting in triangles and matching triangle colours to the end 2 triangles on the right side of back.

SHAPE NECK: Dec 1 st on left side of work beg next row and every foll 5th row 9(10:11) times in all and AT THE SAME TIME cont to match back. K a few rows with WY and remove from machine.

RIGHT FRONT

Work as Left Front, reversing shaping and placing triangles on to work exactly the same as on left front, except the top triangle, which is 'D' instead of 'F'.

Join shoulders: With P/S of back facing, replace sts on to machine, discarding WY. With K/S of fronts facing, place sts on top of back sts, leaving 20(22:24) sts in centre. With MC K 1 row across all sts. Cast off.

SLEEVES

Push 27(31:35) ndls to WP. Set machine for K1 P1 rib. With MC, cast on selvedge. TD MT -3 RC 000. Rib 10 rows. Hook up to main bed, inc 1 st on L to centre work. TD MT RC 000. Shape sides by inc 1 st each end of 5th and every foll 5th row 5 times, then every 10th row 5 times and AT THE SAME TIME work in patt as follows: [With MC, K 2 rows, with G, K 2 rows] 2(3:4) times. K 2 rows MC. Place an 'F' triangle on to ndl 5 on L and ndl 5 on R. Knit in as before, working in patt as back, placing three more triangles in the centre of the sleeve in the same order as the centre back triangles. Cont to RC 70(74:78). [With G, K 2 rows, with MC, K 2 rows] 2(3:4) times. 48(52:56) sts (see note). Cast off.

BUTTON BAND

Push 11 ndls to WP. Set machine for K1 P1 rib. With MC, cast on selvedge. TD MT -3 RC 000. Rib 96(104:120) rows. Cast off.

Make buttonhole band the same, with buttonholes on RC 4, 19, 34 and 49.

MAKING UP

Sew on button bands to centre back neck, join back seam. If you haven't joined sleeves on the machine, then sew in to the markers. Sew sleeve and side seams. Sew on buttons. Press seams according to the instructions on the ball band and keep one ball band for washing instructions.

**DESIGNER TIP:
Before you begin, try out the technique of knitting in the triangles to ensure a good result when you make this garment.**

TOKYO

Oriental simplicity and economy of line are combined in this tantalizingly inscrutable cotton knit.

TOKYO

MACHINE
Chunky.

MATERIALS
Rowan Yarns Hand Knit Cotton. 50 gm balls.
13(14:15) balls No: 282.

TENSION
Main Tension Dial approx No: 2
19 sts and 28 rows – 10 cm (4in) square, measured over st. st.

MEASUREMENTS
To fit bust:
81–86.5 (91.5–96.5:
101.5–106.5) cm
32–34(36–38:40–42) in
Actual size:
96.5(106.5:117) cm
38(42:46) in
Length:
53(56:58.5) cm
21(22:23) in
Sleeve seam:
30.5 cm
12 in

ABBREVIATIONS
(see page 7)

NOTES
Photographed garment knitted to second size.
NB: Knit side is right side.

BACK
Push 69(79:89) ndls to WP. Set machine for K1 P1 rib. Cast on selvedge. TD MT -2 RC 000. Rib 22 rows. Hook up to main bed, inc 1 st on L to centre work. TD MT RC 000. Shape sides by inc 1 st each end of 7th and every foll 7th row and AT THE SAME TIME work in patt as follows: K to RC 34. ** On R of centre transfer st No: 1 on to st No: 2 and st No: 3 on to st No: 4. Rep on L with only st No: 2 on to st No: 1. K 2 rows. On R of centre transfer st No: 2 on to 3 and 4 on to 5. On L of centre transfer st No: 3 on to 2 and 1 on to 1 on R of centre. K 2 rows. On R, transfer st No: 1 on to 2, 3 on to 4 and 5 on to 6. On L, transfer st No: 2 on to 1 and 4 on to 3. K 2 rows, cont in this way adding 1 more st each time to RC 46 (see Chart). (8 eyelets).
Next row: On R transfer st 7 on to 8, 9 on to 10. On L transfer st 8 on to 7 and 6 on to 5. K 2 rows.
Next row: On R transfer st No: 8 on to 9 and 10 on to 11. On L transfer st No: 9 on to 8 and 7 on to 6. K 2 rows. RC 50.
* Next row: On R, transfer st 7 on to 8, 9 on to 10 and 11 on to 12. On L transfer st 10 on to 9, 8 on to 7, and 6 on to 5.
Cross cables as follows: On L, drop st 5 off ndl and down 4 rows, K up with latch tool as a P st. Rep with st 1 and 6 on R. With two, one-prong tools, remove sts 3 and 4 on L, cross 4 behind 3 and replace on the empty ndls. Rep with sts 1 and 2, crossing 2 behind 1. On R, rep with sts 2 and 3, crossing 3 behind 2. Rep with sts 4 and 5, crossing 5 behind 4. K 4 rows*. These 4 rows form the patt. Rep from * to * throughout. Cont to RC 80. 90 (100:110) sts.
SHAPE RAGLAN: Keeping patt correct, cast off 6(4:2) sts beg next 2 rows, 2 sts beg next 4 rows. With a three-prong tool, to make a fully-fashioned shaping, dec 1 st each end of next row and every alt row. K to RC 116(122:128). 40(48:56) sts. Dec 1 st on R.

YOKE: Transfer sts for K1 P1 rib. Set machine, put in comb and weights. TD MT -1 rib 4 rows. TD MT -1 • rib 4 rows. TD MT- 1 •• rib 4 rows. TD MT -2 rib 10 rows. Rib 1 row TD 6. Cast off.

FRONT
Work as back until 40(48:56) sts rem when shaping raglan. K several rows with WY and remove from machine.

SLEEVES
Push 47(53:57) ndls to WP. Set machine for K1 P1 rib. TD MT – 2 RC 000. Rib 22 rows. Hook up to main bed, inc 1 st on L to centre work TD MT RC 000. Shape sides by inc 1 st each end of 4th and every foll 5th row and AT THE SAME TIME K to RC 14. Cont with incs and work as back from ** to RC 60. 72(78:82) sts.
SHAPE RAGLAN: Cont with patt working raglan shaping as back to RC 96(102:108). 26 sts remain. K several rows with WY and remove from machine.

YOKE
With W/S facing, place 26 sts from first sleeve on machine, then 40(48:56) sts from front and 26 sts from second sleeve. Set machine for K1 P1 rib, transfer sts, dec 1 st at one end. Put in comb and hang weights. Work as back yoke.

MAKING UP
Sew up the raglan seams and back yoke seams. Sew side and sleeve seams. Press according to the instructions on the ball band and keep one ball band for washing instructions.

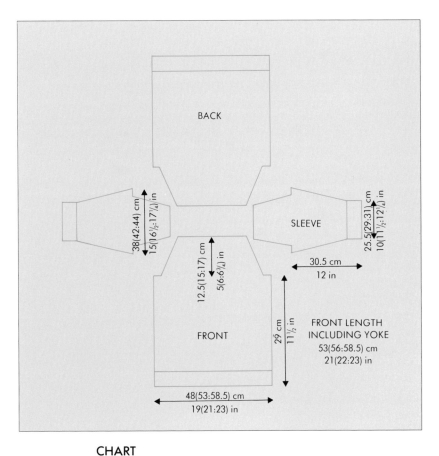

BACK

SLEEVE

38(42:44) cm
15(16½:17¼) in

25.5(29:31) cm
10(11½:12¼) in

12.5(15:17) cm
5(6:6¾) in

30.5 cm
12 in

FRONT

29 cm
11½ in

FRONT LENGTH
INCLUDING YOKE
53(56:58.5) cm
21(22:23) in

48(53:58.5) cm
19(21:23) in

CHART

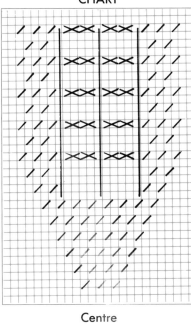

Centre

/   Transfer st to R

✕   Cross 1 st behind the other
as given in patt

| Drop st down and pick up as
a P st on R/S of work

DESIGNER TIP:
Wax the yarn and
always ensure that the
end needles are knitting
each time. Sew shirring
elastic through the first
3 or 4 rows of the welt,
cuffs and yoke to ensure
the rib remains taut.

MISTRAL

**Brave the elements in this cosy sweater,
knitted in an unusual pastel colour
combination.**

MISTRAL

MACHINE
Standard Gauge 24 st punchcard.

MATERIALS
Rowan Yarns Lightweight DK. 500 gm cones.
D 1 cone No: 61
E 1 cone No: 59
F 1 cone No: 8
H 1 cone No: 502
J 1 cone No: 89
G 1 cone No: 20
   3 buttons.

TENSION
Main Tension Dial approx No: 10
30 sts and 34 rows – 10 cm (4 in) square, measured over pattern.

MEASUREMENTS
To fit chest:
  91.5(96.5:101.5:106.5.112) cm
  36(38:40:42:44) in
Actual size:
  106.5(112:117:122:127) cm
  42(44:46:48:50) in
Length:
  68.5(71:74:74:74) cm
  27(28:29:29:29) in
Sleeve length:
  47 cm
  18½ in

ABBREVIATIONS
(see page 7)

NOTES
Photographed garment knitted to fourth size.
NB: Knit side is right side.
Punch cards illustrated before starting to knit.

PATTERN 1
With the first colour in feeder 1/A and the second colour in feeder 2/B, K as follows: 2 rows G/H, 8 rows D/E, 2 rows G/J, 8 rows D/E, 2 rows F/J, 8 rows D/E, 2 rows F/H, 8 rows D/E.
  These 40 rows form the patt.

PATTERN 2
With the first colour in feeder 1/A and the second colour in feeder 2/B, K as follows: 1 row G/H, 4 rows D/E, 1 row G/J, 4 rows D/E, 1 row F/J, 4 rows D/E, 1 row F/H, 4 rows D/E.
  These 20 rows form the patt.

BACK
Lock card 1 on row 1.
NB: Mark each end of row 98(108:116:116:114) with WY.
Push 161(167:175:181:189) ndls to WP. Set machine for K1 P1 rib. With D, cast on selvedge. TD MT -3 RC 000. Rib 30 rows. Hook up to main bed, inc 1 st to L to centre work. TD MT RC 000. K 1 row setting machine for patt. Unlock card, K in pattern 1 to RC192(202: 212:212:212).
  SHAPE SHOULDERS: Lock card (see note). With D, cast off 9(10:11:11:13) sts beg next 2 rows, 10(10:11:11:12) sts beg next 4 rows, 10(10:11:12:12) sts beg next 2 rows and 10(11:11:12:12) sts beg next 4 rows.
  Cast off rem 44 sts.

FRONT
Work as back to RC 150(160: 170:170:170). Carr R.
  SHAPE NECK: Slip the centre 6 sts and all rem sts on opp side to carr on to WY, remove from machine. Cont in pattern 1 to RC 173(183:193:193:193). * Cast off 6 sts beg next row and the foll sts on every alt row 4, 3, 2, 1, 1, 1, 1. Cont straight to RC 192(202:212: 212:212). (K one row more on other side.)
  SHAPE SHOULDER: Lock card, with D cast off 9(10:11:11:13) sts beg next row. K 1 row. Cast off 10(10:11:11:12) sts beg next row and foll alt row. K 1 row, cast off 10(10:11:12:12) sts beg next row, K 1 row, cast off rem 10(11:11:12:12) sts. Reset RC to 150 (160:170:170:170). Replace sts on WY on to machine, over the same ndls as before. Replace card 1 with card 2, locked on row 1. (See manual for resetting ndls.) Carr R. Unlock card. Cast off the first 6 sts.

K in pattern 2 to RC 174(184:194: 194:194). Work neck and shoulder shaping from * to match first side.

RIGHT SLEEVE
Lock card 1 on row 1.
Push 84(84:88:88:92) ndls to WP. Cast on with WY and K a few rows. TD MT RC 000. With D, K 1 row, setting machine for pattern **. Unlock card, K in pattern 1, shaping sides by inc 1 st each end of 3rd and every foll 3rd row, cont to RC 90. Replace card 1 with card 2, locked on row 1. Reset ndls, cont to inc as set, K in pattern 2 to RC 131. 166(166:170:170:174) sts (see note). Cast off.

LEFT SLEEVE
Lock card 2 on row 1.
Work to ** on Right Sleeve. Unlock card, K in pattern 2, shaping sides by inc 1 st each end of 3rd and every foll 3rd row to RC 40. Replace card 2 with card 1, locked on row 1. Reset ndls, cont to inc as set, K in pattern 1 to RC 132. Complete as Right Sleeve.

CUFFS
Push 63(63:67:67:69) ndls to WP. Set machine for K1 P1 rib. With D, cast on selvedge. TD MT -3 RC 000. Rib 30 rows. Hook up to main bed. With W/S sleeve facing, place sts from first row, on to cuff sts as follows: [Place 2 sts on first ndl and 1 st on each of the next 2 ndls] along row. K 1 row loosely by hand, cast off.

COLLAR
Push 141 ndls to WP. Set machine for K1 P1 rib. With D, cast on selvedge. TD MT -1 RC 000. Rib 34 rows (see note). Cast off.

BUTTON BAND
Push 11 ndls to WP. Set machine for K1 P1 rib. With D, cast on selvedge. TD MT -3 RC 000. Rib 26 rows. Cast off. Buttonhole band: Work as button band, making a 2 st buttonhole (see note and manual) on rows 5, 14 and 22.

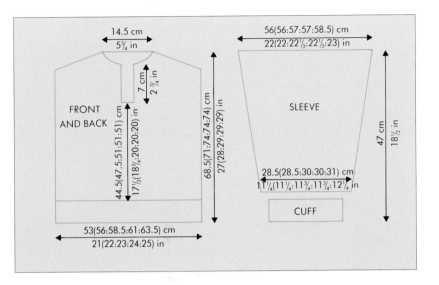

FRONT AND BACK

14.5 cm
5³/₄ in

7 cm
2¹/₄ in

44.5(47.5:51:51:51) cm
17¹/₂(18³/₄:20:20:20) in

68.5(71:74:74:74) cm
27(28:29:29:29) in

53(56:58.5:61:63.5) cm
21(22:23:24:25) in

SLEEVE

56(56:57:57:58.5) cm
22(22:22¹/₂:22¹/₂:23) in

47 cm
18¹/₂ in

28.5(28.5:30:30:31) cm
11¹/₄(11¹/₄:11³/₄:11³/₄:12¹/₄) in

CUFF

MAKING UP

If you have joined shoulders, button bands, collar and sleeves to body on the machine then sew sleeve and side seams. Sew on buttons. If sewing garment by hand, then join shoulders with a flat seam. Sew on button bands, sew cast off edge of collar around neckline and over 6 sts on each button band. Sew sleeves into markers on front and back, sew sleeve and side seams. Sew on buttons. Press seams with a damp cloth, then press the whole garment. Hand wash only in soap flakes, 30°C. Short spin, ease to shape dry flat, away from direct sunlight.

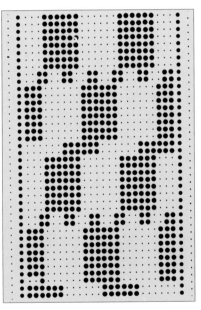

CARD 1

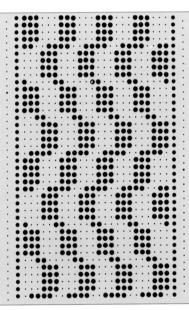

CARD 2

DESIGNER TIP:
Don't cut the contrast yarns when the rows are completed. Loop them over the end needles every 3 rows so that they knit in on the next repeat.

MONO

Double impact with two subtle colourways in the same attractive Fair Isle design.

MONO

MACHINE
Standard Gauge 24 st punchcard.

MATERIALS
Pingouin Pingolaine. 50 gm balls.

	MANS	WOMANS	
5(6:6:7) balls No:	15	35	MC
3(3:3:4) balls No:	62	15	D
2(2:3:3) balls No:	63	62	E
1(1:1:1) balls No:	35	63	F
1(1:1:1) balls No:	74	74	G

TENSION
Main Tension Dial approx No: 8
32 sts and 42 rows - 10 cm (4 in)
square, measured over pattern.

MEASUREMENTS
To fit bust/chest sizes:
81-86.5(91.5-96.5:101.5-
106.5:112-117) cm
32-34(36-38:40-42:44-46) in
Actual size:
91.5(101.5:112:122) cm
36(40:44:48) in
Length:
56(58.5:61:63.5) cm
22(23:24:25) in
Sleeve length:
44.5(44.5:47:49.5) cm
17½(17½: 18½:19½) in

ABBREVIATIONS
(see page 7)

NOTES
Photographed garments knitted to
second and fourth sizes.
NB: Knit side is right side.
Punch cards illustrated before
starting to knit.

BACK
Lock card 1 on row 1.
NB: Mark each end of row
94(88:82:76).
Push 143(159:175:191) ndls to
WP. Set machine for K1 P1 rib.
With MC, cast on selvedge. TD
MT-3 RC 000. Rib 30 rows. Hook
up to main bed, inc 1 st on L to
centre work. TD MT RC 000. K 1 row,
setting machine for patt. Unlock
card. With MC in feeder 1/A and D
in feeder 2/B, K12(18:22:28) rows.
Replace card 1 with card 2 locked
on row 1. With MC, K 2 rows
setting machine for patt on last
row. Unlock card. RC 000. With the
first colour in feeder 1/A and the
second colour in feeder 2/B, K as
follows: 1 row MC/-, 6 rows MC/D,
2 rows -/D, 3 rows E/D, 4 rows
E/MC, 1 row G/MC, 4 rows E/MC,
3 rows E/D, 2 rows -/D, 6 rows
MC/D, 2 rows MC/-, 1 row MC/G,
2 rows MC/-, 6 rows MC/F, 1 row
E/F, 6 rows MC/F, 2 rows MC/-, 1
row MC/G, 1 row MC/-. These 54
rows form the patt. Cont in patt to
RC 169.
   Replace card 2 with card 1,
locked on row 1. K 2 rows with MC,
setting machine for patt. Unlock
card, K to RC 178(182:186:190). K
a few rows with WY, and remove
from machine.

FRONT
Work as back to RC 90.
   SHAPE NECK: On opp side to
carr, slip all sts from centre 0 on to
WY and remove from machine.
Card row No: 37. Work on first set
of sts to match back, dec 1 st at
neck edge on next and every foll
4th row 20(22:22:24) times. Cont
straight to RC 178(182:186:190). K
a few rows with WY and remove
from machine. Replace sts on WY
on to machine for second side of
neck, on to the same ndls as before.
Reset card and ndls (see manual).
Work to match first side.
   Join shoulders: With R/S of work
facing, place back sts on to machine.
With W/S of front facing, place front
shoulder sts on top of back sts,
leaving 40(44:44:48) sts in centre
back neck. TD 10. K 1 row across
all sts. Cast off.

SLEEVES
Lock card 1 on row 1.
Push 87(95:95:103) ndls to WP. Set
machine for K1 P1 rib. With MC,
cast on selvedge. TD MT -4 RC
000. Rib 30 rows. Hook up to main
bed, inc 1 st on L to centre work. TD
MT RC 000. Shape sides by inc 1 st
each end of 12th(2nd:12th:2nd)
row, then every foll 6th(6th:4th:4th)
row and AT THE SAME TIME work
in patt as follows: K 1 row with MC,
setting machine for patt. Unlock
card. With MC in feeder 1/A and D
in feeder 2/B, K12(12:18:18) rows.
Replace card 1 with card 2 locked
on row 1. With MC, K 1 row, setting
carr for patt, unlock card and work
in patt as back to RC 120(120:
128:128).
   Replace card 2 with card 1,
locked on row 1. K 1 row with MC,
setting carr for patt, unlock card.
With MC in feeder 1/A and D in
feeder 2/B, K12(18:18:22) rows,
cont to inc as set to 128(144:
160:176) sts (see note). Cast off.

NECKBAND
BACK: Push 41(45:45:49) ndls to
WP. Set machine for K1 P1 rib.
With MC, cast on selvedge. TD
MT -4 RC 000. Rib 12 rows. Hook
up to main bed (see note). Cast off.
FRONT: (2 pieces alike) Push
81(83:85:87) ndls to WP, work as
given for back.

MAKING UP
If you have joined neckband and
sleeves to front and back on the
machine, cont as follows. Join
sleeve and side seams. If you are
sewing garment by hand, sew in
sleeves to markers. Sew cast off
edge of neckbands on to neckline.
Mitre the vee, by folding to the
inside the ends of the two bands, to
form a diamond, and sew the row-
ends up the side of the band. Sew
together the two bands at centre
front. Join side and sleeve seams.
Press according to the instructions
on the ball band and keep one ball
for washing instructions.

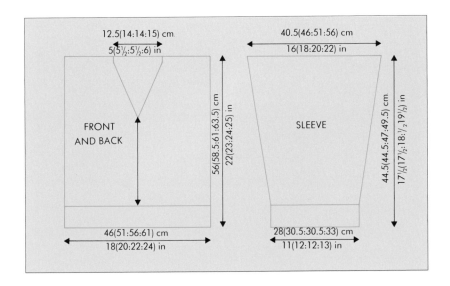

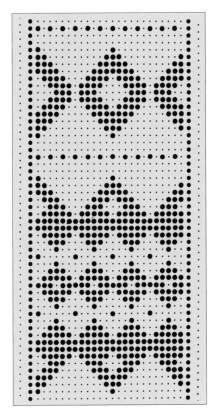

CARD 2

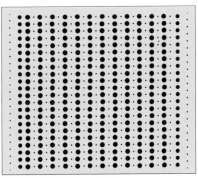

CARD 1

DESIGNER TIP:
Mitring the neckband in the way I have described eliminates the need for decreasing as you make the rib and gives a neater finish.

FLOATING

A simple technique creates a ravishing sweater in downy-soft angora.

FLOATING

MACHINE
Standard Gauge 24 st punchcard.

MATERIALS
Jaeger Angora Spun. 20 gm balls.
C   10(12) balls No: 558
D   3 balls No: 564
E   3 balls No: 586
F   3 balls No: 587

TENSION
Main Tension Dial approx No: 8
31 sts and 42 rows – 10 cm (4 in)
square, measured over pattern.

MEASUREMENTS
To fit bust:
   86.5 – 96.5(101.5 – 112) cm
   34–38(40–44) in
Actual size:
   101.5(117) cm
   40(46) in
Length:
   59.5 cm
   23½ in

ABBREVIATIONS
(see page 7)

NOTES
Photographed garment knitted to
first size.
NB: Purl side is right side.
Punch card illustrated before
starting to knit.

BACK
NB: Mark each end of row 120.
Lock card on row 1. Push 157(181)
ndls to WP. Set machine for K1 P1
rib. With C, cast on selvedge. TD
MT –2 RC 000. Rib 34 rows. Hook
up to main bed, inc 1 st on L to
centre work. TD MT K 1 row, setting
machine for patt. Unlock card. RC
000. With the first colour in feeder
1/A and the second colour in
feeder 2/B, K as follows: ** 12 rows
D/C. * On R of centre 0, with 2
prong tool, take st Nos: 72 and 73
off ndls and on to tool. Bring tool
under and over the top of the floats
and replace sts on to the empty
ndls. Rep over st Nos: 60/61,
48/49, 36/37, 24/25, 12/13 and
on second size over st Nos: 84/85.
Rep over same sts on L of centre.
Rep over st No: 1 on L and 1 on R.
Replace ndls in correct position *. K
12 rows E/C, rep from * to *. K 12
rows F/C, rep from * to *. K 12 rows
D/C, rep from * to *. K 12 rows
E/C, rep from * to *. K 12 rows F/C,
rep from * to *, **.Rep from ** to **.
Cont in pattern to RC 180. Card
row 37.
   SHAPE NECK: Slip the centre 82
sts and all rem sts on opp side to
carr on WY and remove from
machine. Cont in pattern on the
first set of sts as set to RC 216. K a
few rows with WY and remove from
machine. Leave the centre 82 sts on
WY, replacing the rem sts on to the
same ndls as before. Reset RC, card
and ndls (see manual), K to match
first side.

FRONT
Work exactly as back, but reversing
colours, and leaving the second
shoulder sts on the machine. With
the K/S of back facing, place back
shoulder sts on top of front
shoulder sts. TD 10. K 1 row with C,
cast off. Discard WY. Rep with rem
shoulder.

YOKE
Push 85 ndls to WP. Set machine
for K1 P1 rib. With C, cast on
selvedge. TD MT RC 000. Rib 36
rows. Hook up to main bed. With
K/S of back facing, place the 82 sts
on WY on to rib sts, leaving 1 rib st
at one side, and 2 sts at other side.
K 1 row TD 10. Cast off.
   Rep on front.

ARMBAND
(2 pieces alike)
Push 189 ndls to WP. Set machine
for K1 P1 rib. With C, cast on
selvedge. TD MT–2 RC 000. Rib 80
rows. Cast off.

BOW
Push 31 ndls to WP. Set machine
for K1 P1 rib. With C, cast on
selvedge. TD MT –2 RC 000. Rib 30
rows. Cast off. Gather up across
row 15.

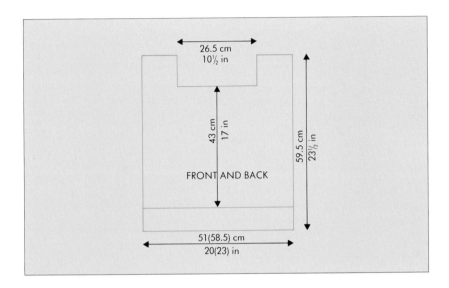

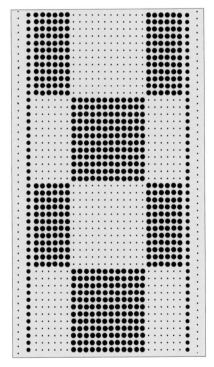

MAKING UP

Sew sides of yoke on to front. Rep on back. Attach bow to centre front. Sew cast off edge of armbands on to front and back between the markers. Sew under seam on armband, reversing half-way for turn back cuff. Sew side seams. Press according to instructions on the ball band and keep one ball band for washing instructions.

DESIGNER TIP:
Don't be discouraged by the complex appearance of this attractive design. Knitting a sample swatch will show how easy the technique is in reality.

RAMBLER

Cuddle up in this cosy cardigan and you won't mind if you *do* get lost on your travels.

RAMBLER

MACHINE
Chunky.

MATERIALS
Hayfield Lugano Plain. 50 gm balls.
12(13:14) balls No: 058.
4 buttons.

TENSION
Main Tension Dial approx No: 3
20 sts and 24 rows - 10 cm (4in) square, measured over st.st.

MEASUREMENTS
To fit bust:
81–86.5(91.5–96.5:101.5–106.5) cm
32–34(36–38:40–42) in
Actual size:
91.5(101.5:112) cm
36(40:44) in
Length:
73.5(76:79) cm
29(30:31) in
Sleeve length:
42 cm
16½ in

ABBREVIATIONS
(see page 7)

NOTES
Photographed garment knitted to third size.
NB: Knit side is right side.

BACK
NB: Mark each end of row 76 with WY.
Push 92(102:112) ndls to WP. Set machine for K2 P2 rib. Cast on selvedge. TD MT RC 000. Rib 40 rows. Hook up to main bed. RC 000. K to RC 132(138:144).
   SHAPE SHOULDERS: * On opp side to carr, push the first 6(7:8) sts to HP. Set carr for partial knitting. K 1 row. Push one more st to HP, adjacent to those already in HP. Rep from * 9 times more. [On opp side to carr push the 35(40:45) sts in HP, to WP. K 1 row] twice. K several rows with WY, remove from machine.

LEFT FRONT
Pocket Lining: Push 20(22:24) ndls to WP. With 'e' wrap method, cast on. TD MT RC 000. K 48 rows. K several rows with WY, remove from machine. Push 42(46:52) ndls to WP. Set machine for K2 P2 rib. Cast on selvedge TD MT RC 000. Rib 40 rows. Hook up to main bed, inc 1 st on L on second size only. 42(47:52) sts. RC 000. K 48 rows.
   Pocket: Leave the first 11(12:14) sts nearest carr. Take the next 20(22:24) sts off machine on WY. With W/S of pocket lining facing, place the last row on to the empty ndls. Discard WY. Cont to RC 72.
   SHAPE NECK: On R, dec 1 st beg next row and every foll 7(8:9) rows until 7 sts dec in all. Cont straight to RC 132(138:144) (K one more row on Right Front). Carr R.
   SHAPE SHOULDER: * On opp side to carr, push the first 6(7:8) sts to HP. Set carr for partial knitting. K 1 row. Push one more st to HP, adjacent to those already in HP. K 1 row. Rep from * until 28(32:36) sts in HP. Reset carr for knitting. K 1 row across all sts. With R/S of back facing, place the left shoulder sts on top of front shoulder sts. Discard WY. K 4 rows. Cast off.

POCKET TOP
Push 20(22:24) ndls to WP. Set machine for K2 P2 rib. Cast on selvedge. TD MT Rib 6 rows. Hook up to main bed. With W/S front facing, place the sts on WY on top of rib sts. Cast off.

RIGHT FRONT
Work as Left Front, reversing shaping.

SLEEVES
Push 52(56:60) ndls to WP. Set machine for K2 P2 rib. Cast on selvedge. TD MT -2 RC 000. Rib 24 rows. Hook up to main bed. TD MT RC 000. Shape sides by inc 1 st each end of 1st(6th:3rd) row and every foll 4th(3rd:3rd) row 19(22:25) times in all. 90(100:110) sts. Cont to RC 80. Take the back and fronts and with R/S work facing, place a st from each side of the shoulder seam (at sleeve edge) onto the centre 2 sts. Take a loop from the row-ends between the markers, placing them on to the sleeve sts. K 4 rows. Cast off.

BUTTON BAND AND COLLAR
Button Band and left side of collar: Push 40 ndls to WP. Set machine for K2 P2 rib. Cast on selvedge. Carr L. TD MT RC 000. Rib 16 rows. Set carr for partial knitting. On opp side to carr place a marker yarn over the end ndl.
   ** Push 5 sts to HP, rib 1 row. Push one more st to HP, rib 1 row. Rep from ** until 10 sts remain in WP. Reset carr for knitting. RC 000. Rib 5 rows across all sts. Dec 1 st on same side as marker yarn on next row and every foll 4th row 8 times, then on 3rd and every foll 3rd row 8 times, then every alt row 8 times. 16 sts remain. RC 000. Rib 83(85:87) rows. Cast off. Buttonhole Band: Starting with carr on opp side, work as button band until 16 sts remain. Cont straight making a 2 st buttonhole (see note and manual) on RC 6, 31, 56, and 81.

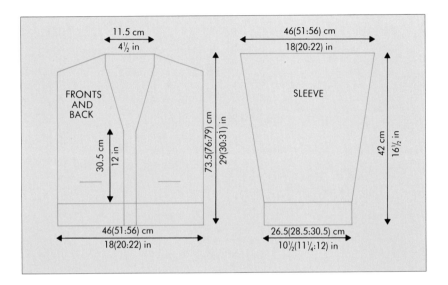

FRONTS
AND
BACK

11.5 cm
4½ in

30.5 cm
12 in

73.5(76:79) cm
29(30:31) in

46(51:56) cm
18(20:22) in

SLEEVE

46(51:56) cm
18(20:22) in

42 cm
16½ in

26.5(28.5:30.5) cm
10½(11¼:12) in

MAKING UP

Sew sleeve and side seams, omitting welt. Sew pocket linings and ends of pocket tops. Sew button band onto left front, with marker yarn at shoulder seam. Rep on right front with buttonhole band. Join centre back seam on collar. Sew on buttons. Brush all over with teazel brush, keep one ball band for washing instructions.

DESIGNER TIP:
Always give work a slight tug every few rows to release the pile from the machine.

LEXICON

The colourful panels on this sweater spell schoolday fun for everyone!

LEXICON

MACHINE
Standard Gauge 24 st punchcard.

MATERIALS
Patons Diploma 4 Ply. 50 gm balls.
C   6(6:7:7) balls No: 4713
D   1 ball No: 4732
E   1 ball No: 4736
F   1 ball No: 4750
    2 studs.

TENSION
Main Tension Dial approx No: 8
30 sts and 39 rows – 10 cm (4 in)
square, measured over st.st.

MEASUREMENTS
To fit chest:
    61 (66:71:76) cm
    24(26:28:30) in
Actual size:
    66 (71:76:81) cm
    26 (28:30:32) in
Length:
    40.5(43:46:48) cm
    16(17:18:19) in
Sleeve seam:
    33(35.5:38:40.5) cm
    13(14:15:16) in

ABBREVIATIONS
(see page 7)

NOTES
Photographed garment knitted to
third size.
NB: Purl side is right side.
Punch cards illustrated before
starting to knit.

PATCHES
Make 3 Geese, 3 Waders and 2 of
each of the alphabets.

GOOSE
Lock card 1 on row 1.
* Push 24 ndls to WP. With WY,
cast on and K a few rows. K 2 rows
C, setting carr for patt on 2nd row.
Unlock card, with the first colour in
feeder 1/A and the second colour
in feeder 2/B, K in patt as follows:
* K 5 rows C/D, 21 rows C/F. Lock
card. K 2 rows C. K several rows

with WY and remove from
machine.

WADER
Lock card 2 on row 1.
Work as Goose from * to *. K 11
rows C/D, 21 rows C/F. Lock card.
K 2 rows C. K several rows with WY
and remove from machine.

ALPHABET 1
Lock card 3 on row 1.
Work as Goose from * to *. K 18
rows C/E, 2 rows C/–, 3 rows C/F, 2
rows C/–, 14 rows C/D, 2 rows C/–,
3 rows C/F, 2 rows C/–, 14 rows
C/E. Lock card. K 2 rows C. K
several rows with WY and remove
from machine.

ALPHABET 2
Lock card 4 on row 1. Work as
Goose from * to *. K 14 rows C/E,
2 rows C/–, 3 rows C/F, 2 rows C/–,
10 rows C/D, 2 rows C/–, 3 rows
C/F, 2 rows C/–, 18 rows C/E. Lock
card. K 2 rows C. K several rows
with WY and remove from
machine. Sew ends horizontally
into patches. Press according to the
instructions on the ball band, being
careful not to distort fabric.

BACK
NB: Mark each end of row
78(82:86:90).
Push 99(107:115:123) ndls to WP.
Set machine for K1 P1 rib. With C,
cast on selvedge. TD MT –3 RC
000. Rib 26 rows. Hook up to main
bed, inc 1 st on L to centre work. TD
MT RC 000. K 6(6:8:10) rows. With
P side of Goose patch facing, take
the first row, and discarding WY,
slip the sts on to ndl Nos: 7 – 30 on
L of centre. Let it drop. K 2 rows.
Take the end st of third row of
Goose patch and place a loop
from this st on to ndl No: 7 and on
the other side on ndl No: 30. K 2
rows. Cont knitting in the patch
every 2 rows. Cont to RC 14(14:
16:18).
    Take Alphabet 2 patch and
introduce in the same way as
Goose over ndl Nos: 5 – 28 on R
of centre. Knit in both patches as

described to RC 36(36:38:40).
Take last row of Goose patch,
discard WY and slip sts on top of
ndl Nos: 7 – 30. Cont knitting in
Alphabet 2 patch to RC 44(44:
46:48). Take Alphabet 1 patch and
introduce as before over ndl Nos:
17 – 40 on L of centre. Knit in end
sts as described, cont to RC
74(74:76:78). Take last row of
Alphabet 2 patch, discard WY and
slip sts on top of ndl Nos: 5 – 28.
Cont to RC 84(84:86:88). Take
Wader patch, and introduce in the
same way as before over ndl Nos:
12 – 35 on R of centre, discarding
WY. Knit in as before. K to RC
108(108:110:112). Take last row
of Alphabet 1 patch, discard WY
and slip sts on top of ndl Nos: 17 –
40. Cont knitting in Wader to RC
120(120:122:124). Take last row
of Wader, discard WY and slip sts
on top of ndl Nos: 12 – 35. Cont to
RC 126(136:142:150).
    SHAPE SHOULDERS: (see note).
Cast off 7(8:9:10) sts beg next 4
rows, 8(9:9:10) sts beg next 2 rows,
10(10:11:11) sts beg next 2 rows.
Cast off rem 36(38:40:42) sts.

FRONT
Work as back to RC 96(106:
112:120). Carr R.
    SHAPE NECK: On L of centre
take all sts from ndl No: 4 off
machine on WY. K 1 row. Cast off 8
sts at beg next row. Cont on first set
of sts to match back to RC
117(127:133:141). Carr L. Cast off
4 sts beg next row and the foll sts
on every alt row at neck edge:
3(3:3:4); 3(3:4:4); 3(4:4:4); 1.
14(15:16:17) sts dec in all. Cont
straight to RC 126(136:142:150).
    SHAPE SHOULDER: Cast off
7(8:9:10) sts beg next row and foll
alt row. K 1 row. Cast off 8(9:9:10)
sts beg next row. K 1 row. Cast off
rem 10(10:11:11) sts. Replace sts
on WY on to machine. RC 96(106:
112:120). Work to match first
side without casting off the first
8 sts and reversing neck and
shoulder shaping.

LEFT SLEEVE
Push 51(53:57:59) ndls to WP. Set
machine for K1 P1 rib. With C, cast

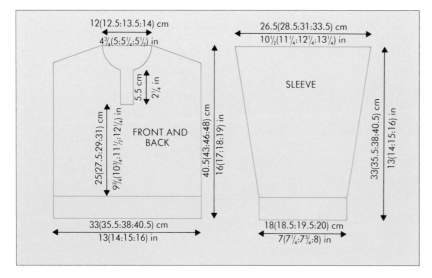

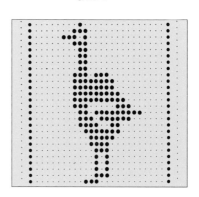

CARD 2

on selvedge. TD MT –3 RC 000. Rib 22 rows. Hook up to main bed, inc 1 st on L to centre work. TD MT RC 000. K 1 row. Shape sides by inc 1 st each end of next and every alt row 4(5:5:5) times, then each end of every foll 9th (9th:8th:7th) row and AT THE SAME TIME work as follows: K to RC 20. Introduce a Wader patch over the centre 24 sts and knit in as given for back. Cont with incs to RC 98(106:114:124). 78(84:92:100) sts (see note).
 Cast off.

RIGHT SLEEVE
Work as left sleeve, omitting Wader patch and introducing a Goose patch over the centre 24 sts on RC 60, knitting in as before.

BUTTON BAND
(2 pieces alike)
Push 13 ndls to WP. Set machine for K1 P1 rib. With C, cast on selvedge. TD MT –3 RC 000. Rib 20 rows. Cast off.

NECKBAND
Push 117(119:121:123) ndls to WP. Set machine for K1 P1 rib. With C, cast on selvedge. TD MT –3 RC 000. Rib 20 rows (see note). Cast off.

MAKING UP
If you have joined shoulders, sleeves and neckband on the machine, then sew sleeve and side seams. Attach studs to button bands. If you are sewing garment by hand then join shoulders with a flat seam. Sew in sleeves, join button bands and neckband. Sew sleeve and side seams. Attach studs to button bands. Press according to

the instructions on the ball band and keep one band for washing instructions.

DESIGNER TIP:
Try out the technique of attaching the decorative patches before you knit them into the actual garment.

CARD 1

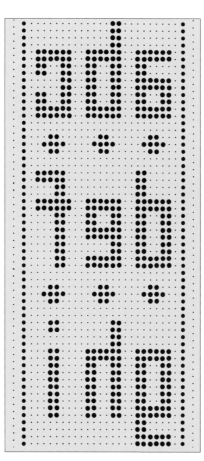

CARD 3

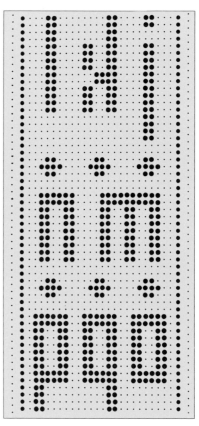

CARD 4

PARISIENNE

A taste of true French city chic with elegant abstract designs on black cotton.

PARISIENNE

MACHINE
Standard Gauge 24 st punchcard.

MATERIALS
Rowan Yarns Soft Cotton. 350 gm cones.
C   1 cone No: 526
D   1 cone No: 527
E   1 cone No: 525
    4 buttons.

TENSION
Main Tension Dial approx No: 6
32 sts and 40 rows – 10 cm (4 in) square, measured over pattern.

MEASUREMENTS
To fit bust:
    86.5–96.5 (96.5–106.5) cm
    34–38(38–42) in
Actual size:
    112(122) cm
    44(48) in
Length:
    56(59.5) cm
    22(23½) in

ABBREVIATIONS
(see page 7)

NOTES
Photographed garment knitted to first size.
NB: Knit side is right side.
Punch cards illustrated before starting to knit.

BACK
Lock card 1 on row 1.
Push 142(154) ndls to WP. With C, cast on with 'e' wrap method. TD MT RC 000. K 1 row, setting machine for patt. Carr L. Unlock card. With C in feeder 1/A and D in feeder 2/B, K 26(36) rows. Replace card 1 with card 2, locked on row 1.
    * With E, K 6 rows. Take the loop of the first st on the first E row and pick up and place on ndl. Rep along row to make a small hem *. Set ndls (see manual) and carr for first row of patt. Unlock card. With C in feeder 1/A and D in feeder 2/B, K 26 rows. Replace card 2 with card 3, locked on row

1. Work from * to *. Set ndls and carr for first row of patt. Unlock card, with C in feeder 1/A and D in feeder 2/B, K 36 rows. Replace card 3 with card 4, locked on row 1. Work from * to *. Set ndls and carr for first row of patt. Unlock card, with C in feeder 1/A and D in feeder 2/B, K 4(6) rows. On opp side to carr push the first 3(15) sts to HP. Set carr for partial knitting. K 1 row, push 1 more st (adjacent to those already in HP) to HP. K 1 row. [Push next 5 sts to HP. K 1 row, push 1 more st to HP, K 1 row] until 12 sts remain in WP. [Push the first 6 sts in HP, nearest carr, to WP, K 2 rows] until 4(16) sts remain. Push these sts to WP. K 4(6) rows. Replace card 4 with card 3 locked on row 1. Work from * to *. Set ndls and carr for first row of patt. Unlock card, with C in feeder 1/A and D in feeder 2/B, K 36 rows. Replace card 3 with card 2, locked on row 1. Work from * to *. Set ndls and carr for first row of patt. Unlock card, with C in feeder 1/A and D in feeder 2/B, K 26 rows. Replace card 2 with card 1 locked on row 1. Work from * to *. Set ndls and carr for first row of patt. Unlock card, with C in feeder 1/A and D in feeder 2/B, K 26(36) rows. Lock card. Cast off.

FRONT
Work exactly as back.

WELT
(Back and front alike)
Push 117(143) ndls to WP. Set machine for K1 P1 rib. With C, cast on selvedge. TD MT –3 RC 000. Rib 36 rows, hook up to main bed. Take the shortest edge of back, and with W/S facing, place a loop from the row-end on to the first st. Cont across back, K 1 row loosely. Cast off.

NECKBAND
(2 pieces alike)
Push 165(199) ndls to WP. Set machine for K1 P1 rib. With C, cast on selvedge TD MT –3. Rib 18 rows, hook up to main bed. Take the longest edge of back, and with W/S facing, place loops evenly from the row-ends on to the rib sts. K 1 row loosely. Cast off.

ARMBAND
(2 pieces alike)
Push 189(199) ndls to WP. Set machine for K1 P1 rib. With C, cast on selvedge TD MT–3. Rib 40 rows. Cast off.

MAKING UP
Overlap neckbands and sew together at outer edges. Sew 2 buttons on right, through both thicknesses of the neckband, rep on left, leaving a 31 cm (12 in) opening in centre. Sew cast off edge of armband on to front and back, sew side and armband seams, turning seam halfway to allow for turn-back cuff. Press patterns with a damp cloth. Hand wash only, in soap flakes, 30°C. Short spin, ease to shape, dry flat away from direct sunlight.

DESIGNER TIP:
Insert knitting needles into the small hems and pull slightly to tighten up the stitches in the garment.

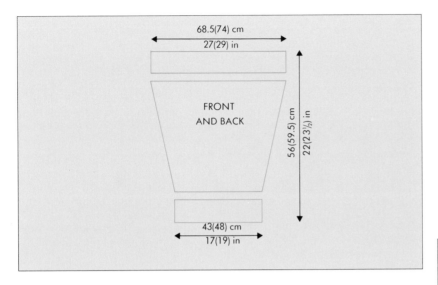

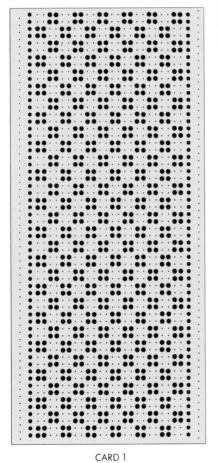

CARD 1

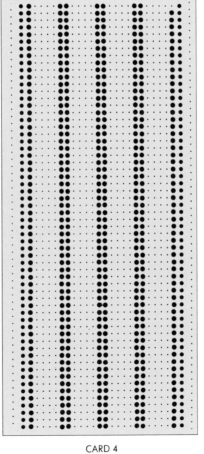

CARD 4

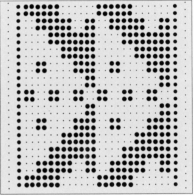

CARD 2

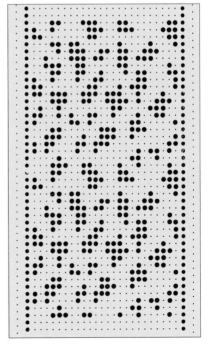

CARD 3

AER○

**Keep cool through the lazy
summer days in this easy-living
cotton top.**

AER○

MACHINE
Standard Gauge.

MATERIALS
Silverknit Marrakesh 4 ply. 200 gm cones.
MC 2 cones No: 10
C   1 cone No: 12

TENSION
Main Tension Dial approx No: 6
30 sts and 44 rows – 10 cm (4 in) square, measured over pattern.

MEASUREMENTS
To fit bust:
  81–86.5(91.5–96.5:101.5–106.5) cm
  32–34(36–38:40–42) in
Actual size:
  94(104:114.5) cm
  37(41:45) in
Length:
  53(53:58.5) cm
  21(21:23) in

ABBREVIATIONS
(see page 7)

NOTES
Photographed garment knitted to second size.
NB: Purl side is right side.

BACK
Push 139(153:167) ndls to WP. Set machine for K1 P1 rib. With MC, cast on selvedge. TD MT –3 RC 000. Rib 34 rows. Hook up to main bed, inc 1 st on L to centre work. TD MT RC 000. K 8(8:18) rows.
  First Block of Eyelets: * Next row: On R of centre 0, transfer st Nos: 65 to 64, leaving empty ndl in WP. In the same way, transfer st Nos: 63 to 62, 61 – 60, 59 – 58, 57 – 56, 55 – 54, 53 – 52, 51 – 50, 49 – 48, 47 – 46, 45 – 44, 11 to 10, 9 – 8, 7 – 6, 5 – 4, 3 – 2, 1 to 1 on L of centre 0. On L of centre transfer st Nos: 2 – 3, 4 – 5, 6 – 7, through to 10 – 11, then 44 – 45, 46 – 47 through to 64 – 65. K 2 rows.
  Next row: On R of centre 0, transfer st Nos: 64 – 63, 62 – 61, through to 46 – 45, then 12 – 11, 10 – 9, through to 2 – 1. On L of centre 0, transfer 1 – 2, 3 – 4, through to 9 – 10, then 43 – 44, through to 63 – 64. K 2 rows *. Rep from * to * (4 rows), 8 more times. RC 44(44:54). K 6 rows to RC 50(50:60).
  Second Block of Eyelets: Next row: On R of centre 0, transfer st Nos: 38 – 37, 36 – 35, through to 18 – 17. On L of centre transfer st Nos: 17 – 18, 19 – 20, through to 37 – 38. K 2 rows. On R of centre, transfer st Nos: 37 – 36, 35 – 34, through to 19 – 18. On L of centre 0, transfer st Nos: 18 – 19, 20 – 21, through to 36 – 37. K 2 rows. Rep last 4 rows, shaping sides on the first two sizes at RC 66(80), by inc 1 st each end of next and every foll alt row. Cont in patt to RC 86(86:96). K 6 rows, cont to inc on first 2 sizes.
  Third Block of Eyelets: Work as First Block of Eyelets, on third size start to inc 1 st each end of next and every foll alt row to RC 94. Cont to inc on all sizes to 192 sts RC 117 (117:127). Complete Third Block of Eyelets. RC 128(128:138). K 6 rows.

  Fourth Block of Eyelets: Transfer sts as first row of Second Block of Eyelets, and also on R of centre 0, st Nos: 92 – 91, 90 – 89, through to 72 – 71. On L of centre 0, st Nos: 71 – 72, 73 – 74, through to 91 – 92. K 2 rows. On R of centre transfer st Nos: 91 – 90, through to 71 – 72, and on L of centre 0, st Nos: 70 – 71, through to 90 – 91, and all sts as Second Block of Eyelets. K 2 rows. Rep last 4 rows 8 times more to RC 170(170:180). Cont straight to RC 200(200:220).
  SHAPE SHOULDERS: (see note). Cast off 10 sts beg next 10 rows and 11 sts beg next 2 rows. Cast off rem 70 sts.

FRONT
Work as back to RC 180(180:200).
  SHAPE NECK: (see p 12). Push the centre 20 sts and all rem sts on opp side to carr to HP. Set carr for partial knitting. K 1 row, slipping yarn under the first ndl in HP. K 2 rows. Cast off 5 sts beg next and foll alt row. K 1 row. Cast off 4 sts beg next row, K 1 row, cast off 3 sts beg next row, K 1 row. Cast off 2 sts beg next and foll alt rows 3 times in all. K 1 row, dec 1 st beg next and foll alt row. (25 sts dec in all.) Cont straight to RC 200 (200:220).
  SHAPE SHOULDER: Cast off 10 sts beg next and foll alt rows 5 times, K 1 row, cast off rem 11 sts. Leaving centre 20 sts in HP, push rem sts to WP. Reset RC. Work to match first side. With a spare piece of yarn, cast off the centre 20 sts.

NECKBAND
Push 159 ndls to WP. Set machine for K1 P1 rib. With MC, cast on selvedge. TD MT –3 RC 000. Rib 11 rows (see p 13). Cast off.

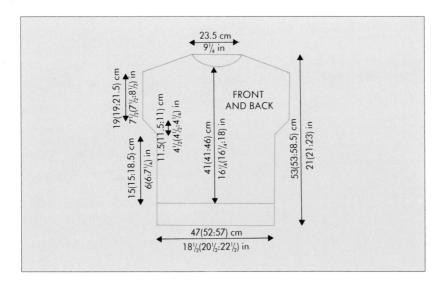

23.5 cm
9¼ in

FRONT
AND BACK

19(19:21.5) cm
7½(7½:8½) in

11.5(11.5:11) cm
4½(4½:4¼) in

41(41:46) cm
16¼(16¼:18) in

53(53:58.5) cm
21(21:23) in

15(15:18.5) cm
6(6:7¼) in

47(52:57) cm
18½(20½:22½) in

ARMBAND
(2 pieces alike)
Push 108(108:118) ndls to WP. Set machine for K1 P1 rib. With MC, cast on selvedge. TD MT –3 RC 000. Rib 11 rows. Cast off.

CORDS
Push 5 ndls to WP. With 'e' wrap method cast on with C. Set carr for knitting in one direction only. TD MT RC 000. K approx 40 rows. The cord should measure approx 12.5 cm (5in). RC 80. Leave a 15 cm (6in) length each end for sewing up. Make 47 more.

MAKING UP
Take one cord, push through the eyelet at top right corner of block. Sew down inside. Rep with the other end of the cord at bottom right eyelet. Take a second cord, push through eyelet at top left. Take it around the first cord, then push through bottom left eyelet and sew down. Rep with every block.

If you have joined shoulder seams and neckband on the machine, sew edges of neckband. If you are sewing garment by hand, join shoulders with a flat seam, sew cast off edge of neckband around neckline. Both methods: Sew cast off edge of armbands on to front and back, from the ends of the armhole incs, stretching to fit. Sew side seams. Press seams with a damp cloth. See instructions on cone for washing.

DESIGNER TIP:
Experienced knitters may want to incorporate the cords into the knitting as they go. A sample swatch will show just how easy this is.

TWISTER

The ideal out-sized cardigan for country rambles – and walking the dog!

TWISTER

MACHINE
Chunky.

MATERIALS
Sunbeam Aran Tweed. 50 gm balls.
  17(18:19) balls No: 80.
  5 wooden buttons.

TENSION
Main Tension Dial approx No: 4
18 sts and 28 rows – 10 cm (4 in) square, measured over st.st.

MEASUREMENTS
To fit bust:
  96.5–101.5(106.5–112:117–122) cm
  38–40(42–44:46–48) in
Actual size:
  106.5(117:127) cm
  42(46:50) in
Length:
  61(63.5:66) cm
  24(25:26) in
Sleeve seam:
  43(44.5:46) cm
  17(17½:18) in

ABBREVIATIONS
(see page 7)

NOTES
Photographed garment knitted to third size.
NB: Purl side is right side.

TWISTS
Push 6 ndls to WP. Cast on with WY, K a few rows. * TD MT RC 000. Change to MC. K 16 rows. Cut off MC, leaving a 10 cm (4 in) length. Replace with WY, K 8 rows. Cut off WY. Rep from * 45 times.
  Cut through the centre of the 8 WY rows.

BACK
Push 93(103:111) ndls to WP. Set machine for K1 P1 rib. Cast on selvedge. TD MT -2 RC 000. Rib 24 rows. Hook up to main bed, inc 1 st on L and on third size also inc 2 sts on R. TD MT RC 000. K 6 rows.
** On R of centre, over ndl Nos: 38–43 inclusive, introduce a twist as follows: With P/S of twist facing place row 1 on to these sts discarding WY, let it drop. Rep on ndl Nos: 18–23. Rep over the same ndl Nos: on L. Place a 5th twist over ndl Nos: 3–1 on L and 1–3 on R. K 14 rows. Taking the first twist, while still dropped down, twist once clockwise so that K/S is facing, then once again so that P/S is facing. Lift up, so that K/S is facing and place on sts, discarding WY. Rep with rem twists. K to RC 40. Rep from **. K to RC 74. Place twists as before only over ndl Nos: 3–1 on L and 1–3 on R and 18–23 on R and L. K 2 rows.
SHAPE RAGLAN: Cast off 8(10:12) sts beg next 2 rows, then dec 1 st each end of 4th and every foll 4th row. K to RC 88, pick up twists as before. Cont with dec as set to RC 108. Place twists over the same ndls as last time, cont with dec as set. K to RC 122. Pick up twists as before. Cont with dec as set to RC 138(144:150). 50(52:56) sts remain. Mark the centre 20(22:24) sts with WY. K several rows with WY and remove from machine.

LEFT FRONT
Pocket Lining: Push 22 ndls to WP. TD MT RC 000. With 'e' wrap method, cast on. K 26 rows. K a few rows with WY, and remove from machine. Push ndl Nos: 4–46(4–52: 4–56) on R of centre to WP. 43(49:53) ndls in WP. Set machine for K1 P1 rib. Cast on selvedge. TD MT -2. RC 000. Rib 24 rows. Hook up to main bed, inc 1 st on R on first and third sizes. 44(49:54) sts. TD MT RC 000. K 6 rows. Place twists on the same ndls as back Nos: 18–23 and 38–43. K 14 rows. Place twist on ndls as before. K to RC 26.
  Pocket: Slip st Nos: 20–41 inclusive on to WY and remove from machine. With P side facing, place pocket lining sts on to the empty ndls, discarding WY. Cont to match back twists throughout, K to RC 68.
SHAPE NECK: On L, dec 1 st beg next row and every foll 8th row 7(8:9) times in all, to RC 76.
SHAPE RAGLAN: Cast off 8(10:12) sts on R, then dec 1 st on 4th and every foll 4th row to RC 138(144:150). 15(15:16) sts remain. With the K side of back facing, place the 15(15:16) back shoulder sts on top and cast off both sets of sts together.
  Make right front to match, reversing shaping.

POCKET TOP
Push 23 ndls to WP. Set machine for K1 P1 rib. Cast on selvedge. TD MT -2. Rib 6 rows. Hook up to main bed, dec 1 st on L. With K/S of pocket sts on WY facing, place sts on top of rib sts, discarding WY. Cast off both sets of sts together.

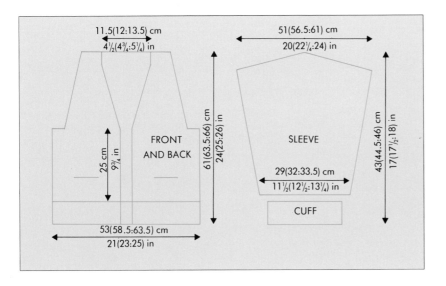

SLEEVES

Push 52(56:60) ndls to WP. Cast on with WY and K a few rows. Change to MC. TD MT RC 000. K 3(3:6) rows. Shape sides by inc 1 st each end of next row and every foll 5(4:3) rows, 11(11:8) times, then every 4th row 8(11:16) times to 90(100:108) sts and AT THE SAME TIME, insert twists over ndl Nos: 3–1 on L and 1–3 on R and 18–23 on R and L on rows 19(21:25). K 14 rows, twist as before. Rep on row 53(55:59), K 14 rows and twist. Rep on row 87(89:93). K 14 rows and twist as before. K 0(3:6) rows straight.

SHAPE TOP: Cast off 4 sts beg next 20(22:24) rows. Cast off rem 10(12:12) sts.

CUFFS

Push 39(41:45) ndls to WP. Set machine for K1 P1 rib. Cast on selvedge. TD MT -2 RC 000. Rib 12 rows. Hook up to main bed. With K/S of sleeve facing, place sts on WY on top of cuff sts as follows. On first and third sizes: *** Place 1 st on each of the first 2 ndls, and 2 sts on next ndl ***. Rep from *** to *** along row. Second size: Place 2 sts on first ndl, then work from *** on first size. Cast off both sets of sts together.

BUTTON BAND

Push 11 ndls to WP. Set machine for K1 P1 rib. Cast on selvedge. TD MT -3 RC 000. Rib 184(190:196) rows. Cast off. Buttonhole Band: Work as button band, making a 2 st buttonhole (see note and manual) on RC 4, 22, 40, 58 and 76.

MAKING UP

Sew down pocket linings and ends of pocket tops. Sew sleeves on to front and back. Sew sleeve and side seams. Sew on bands and buttons. Press all seams, according to the instructions on the ball band and keep one ball band for washing instructions.

DESIGNER TIP:
Pin the front band on to the garment before sewing it on. Hold up the garment to check that its shape is not distorted by the band and adjust accordingly.

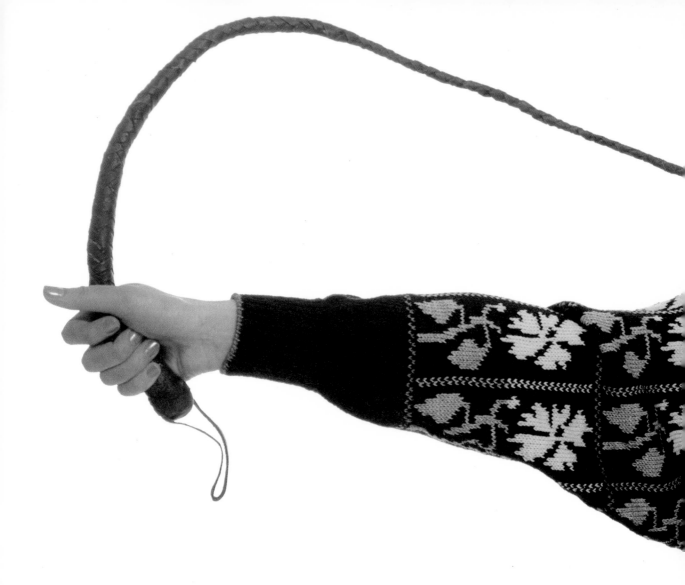

PERENNIAL

Neutral tones add an extra dimension to the bold floral design of this glamorous winter knit.

PERENNIAL

MACHINE
Standard Gauge 24 st punchcard.

MATERIALS
Patons Diploma 4 Ply. 50 gm balls.
C   7(8:8:9) balls No: 4728
D   2 balls No: 4711
E   3 balls No: 4750
G   1 ball No: 4713

TENSION
Main Tension Dial approx No: 9
30 sts and 38 rows - 10 cm (4 in)
square, measured over pattern.

MEASUREMENTS
To fit bust:
    81(86.5:91.5:96.5) cm
    32(34:36:38) in
Actual size:
    101.5(106.5:112:117) cm
    40(42:44:46) in
Length:
    59.5(61:62:63.5) cm
    23½(24:24½:25) in
Sleeve length:
    42(43:44.5:46) cm
    16½(17:17½:18) in

ABBREVIATIONS
(see page 7)

NOTES
Photographed garment knitted to
third size.
Punch card illustrated before
starting to knit.
NB: Knit side is right side.

BACK
Lock card on row 1.
NB: Mark each end of row 100 (all
sizes).
Push 151(157:165:171) ndls to
WP. Set machine for K1 P1 rib.
With G, cast on selvedge. Change
to C. TD MT -3 RC 000. Rib 30
rows. Hook up to main bed, inc 1 st
on L to centre work. TD MT RC 000.
With C, K to RC 8(10:12:14),
setting machine for patt on last row.
    Unlock card, working in patt as
follows: Place the first colour in
feeder 1/A and the second colour
in feeder 2/B. K 2 rows C/G, 1 row
C/-, 26 rows C/D, 29 rows C/E, 1
row C/-, 2 rows C/G, 1 row C/-, 26
rows C/D, 29 rows C/E, 1 row C/-,
2 rows C/G, 1 row C/-, 26 rows
C/D, 29 rows C/E, 1 row C/-, 2
rows C/G. RC 187(189:191:193).
Lock card*. With C, K 8(10:12:14)
rows.
    SHAPE SHOULDERS: (see note).
Cast off 13(14:14:15) sts beg next
2 rows. 13(14:15:15) sts beg next 2
rows. 14(14:15:15) sts beg next 2
rows and 14(14:15:16) sts beg next
2 rows. Cast of rem 44(46:48:50) sts.

FRONT
Work as back to *. With C, K
0(2:4:6) rows.
    SHAPE NECK: (see note). Push
centre 14(16:18:20) sts and all rem
sts on opp side to carr to HP. Set
carr for partial knitting. K 1 row,
putting yarn under the first st in HP.
K 2 rows. Cast off 6 sts beg next
row, 5 sts on foll alt row and 4 sts
on foll alt row. K to RC 195(199:
203:207).
    SHAPE SHOULDER: Cast off
13(14:14:15) sts beg next row
13(14:15:15) sts on foll alt row,
14(14:15:15) on foll alt row. K 1
row. Cast off rem 14(14:15:16) sts.
Leave the centre 14(16:18:20) sts
in HP, push the rem sts to WP. Carr
on opp side to neck. Work as for
first side. Cast off centre sts with a
spare length of MC.

SLEEVES
Lock card on row 1.
Push 84(88:92:96) ndls to WP.
With WY, cast on and K a few rows.
Change to C, TD MT RC 000. K to
RC 12(16:22:26), setting machine for
patt on last row. Unlock card.
Shape sides by inc 1 st each end of
next and every foll 3rd row and AT
THE SAME TIME work in patt as
back to RC 130(134:140:144).
150(158:166:174) sts. Lock card.
With C, K 2 rows (see note).
    Cast off.

CUFFS
Push 57(59:61:63) ndls to WP. Set
machine for K1 P1 rib. With G, cast
on selvedge. Change to C. TD
MT - 3 RC 000. Rib 30 rows, hook
up to main bed. With W/S sleeve
facing, place the sts on WY onto
cuff sts as follows: First size: Place 1
st on first ndl, [place 1 st on next ndl
and 2 sts on next ndl] to last 2 ndls,
placing 1 st on each. Second size:
Place 1 st on first ndl and 2 sts on
next ndl, cont in this way. Third
size: Place 2 sts on first ndl and 1 st
on next ndl, cont in this way. Fourth
size: Place 2 sts on first ndl, [2 sts
on next ndl and 1 st on next ndl] to
last 2 ndls, placing 2 sts on each.
Discard WY, K 1 row loosely and
cast off.

COLLAR
Push 113(117:121:125) ndls to
WP. Set machine for K1 P1 rib.
With G, cast on selvedge. Change
to C. TD MT -3 RC 000. Rib 30
rows. Hook up to main bed (see
note). Cast off.

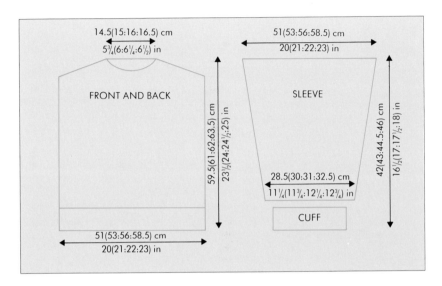

MAKING UP

If you have joined shoulders, collar
and sleeves on machine, sew sleeve
and side seams. If you are sewing
garment by hand, join shoulder
seams with a flat seam, sew in
sleeves to markers, sew cast off
edge of collar around neckline.
Sew sleeve and side seams. Press
according to the instructions on the
ball band, keep one ball band for
washing instructions.

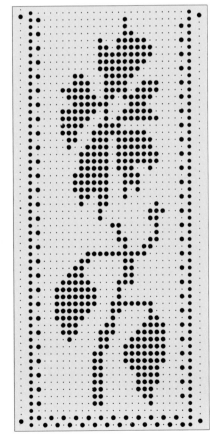

**DESIGNER TIP:
This garment looks
equally stunning when
knitted in a variety of
brilliant colours, so try
ringing the changes.**

PIXE

**Vibrant colours race around
this sweater, bringing a
breath of cheerfulness to
winter days.**

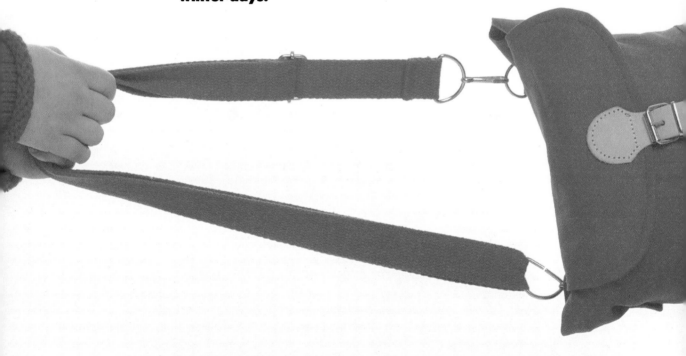

PIXE

MACHINE
Chunky 24 st punchcard.

MATERIALS
Rowan Yarns Aran. 100 gm hanks.
MC 200 gm Red No: 114
E 100(200:200) gm Green No: 112
F 200 gm Black No: 62
D 100 gm Yellow No: 113

TENSION
Main Tension Dial approx No: 4
17 sts and 32 rows – 10 cm (4 in) square, measured over pattern.

MEASUREMENTS
To fit chest:
61(71:81) cm
24(28:32) in
Actual size:
66(76:86.5) cm
26(30:34) in
Length:
42(44.5:47) cm
16½(17½:18½) in
Sleeve seam with cuff rolled:
33(35.5:38) cm
13(14:15) in

ABBREVIATIONS
(see page 7)

NOTES
Photographed garment knitted to third size.
NB: Knit side is right side.
Punch card illustrated before starting to knit.

PATTERN
Pattern consists of 36 rows. With first colour in feeder 1/A, and second colour in feeder 2/B, K 4 rows E/D. * Make a small hem over the centre 6 sts in E as follows: Using transfer tool, pick up a loop from the first row in E and place on ndl above, trapping the long D floats inside hem. Rep until centre 6 sts picked up. Rep over each patt rep *. K 4 rows F/D, rep from * to *. K 4 rows E/D, rep from * to *. With MC K 6 rows. Pattern now repeats, alternating squares as above.

FRONT
Work as back to RC 94(104:108).
    SHAPE NECK: (see note). Set carr for partial knitting. Push centre 12 sts and all rem sts on opp side to carr to HP. K 1 row, slipping yarn under the first st in HP. K 2 rows, cast off the foll sts at neck edge on next and every foll alt row: 2, 2, 2. Cont to RC 100(108:116).
    SHAPE SHOULDER: (On first and second sizes cont to shape neck). Cast off the foll sts at the beg of next and every alt row: 3(4:4), 3(4:5), 3(4:5), K 1 row. Cast off rem 4(4:5) sts. Keeping centre 12 sts in HP, push rem sts into WP. Work as given for first side. Neckband: Push the 12 sts in HP to WP. Push out 10(11:13) ndls each side of centre 12, and pick up an even amount of loops on to these sts up each side of neck. TD MT -1. K 11 rows. Cast off.

WELT
(Back and Front alike)
Push 44(52:56) ndls to WP. With W/S back facing, place the first row on to these ndls dec as follows: First and Third size: [Place 1 st on each of the first 2 ndls, 2 sts on next ndl, 1 st on each of the next 3 ndls and 2 sts on next ndl] to end. Second size: [Place 1 st on each of the first 3 ndls, then 2 sts on next ndl] to end. TD MT -1. With MC, K 22 rows. Cast off.

SLEEVES
Lock card on row 1. Push 28(32:36) ndls to WP. Cast on with WY, K a few rows. TD MT RC 000. Change to MC. K 10(2:6) rows, setting machine for patt on last row. Unlock card. Work in patt, shaping sides by inc 1 st each end of 8th row and every foll 8(9:9) rows to RC 82(90:96). 46(50:54) sts. Cast off.

CUFFS
Push 24(26:28) ndls to WP. With W/S sleeve facing, place the first row on to these ndls, dec as follows. First size: Place 2 sts on each of the first 2 ndls and end 2 ndls, and place 1 st on all rem ndls. Second size: [Place 2 sts on first ndl, 1 st on each of the next 4 ndls] to last ndl, 2 sts on last ndl. Third size: [Place 1 st on each of the first 3 ndls and 2 sts on next ndl] to last 4 ndls, 1 st on each of next 2 ndls and 2 sts on last 2 ndls. TD MT -1. With MC, K 16 rows. Cast off.

BACK
Lock Card on row 19(1:1).
Push 56(64:72) ndls to WP. Cast on with WY, K a few rows. Change to MC. TD MT RC 000. K 10(2:6) rows, setting machine for patt on last row. Unlock card. K in patt to RC 94(104:108). Lock card. With MC cont to RC 100(108:116).
    SHAPE SHOULDERS: (see note). Cast off 3(4:4) sts beg next 2 rows, 3(4:5) sts beg next 6 rows and 4(4:5) sts beg next 2 rows. TD MT -1. On rem 24 sts K 11 rows. Cast off.

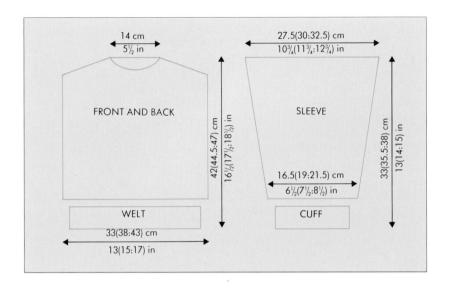

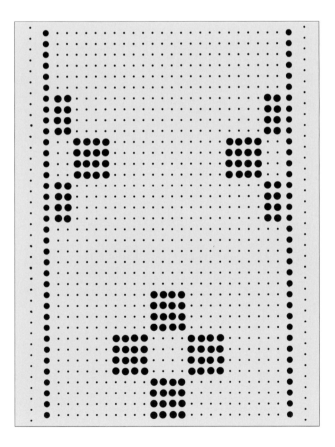

MAKING UP
If you have joined shoulder seams on machine, sew cast off edge of sleeve on to front and back to its full depth, sew sleeve and side seams, turning seams at the cuff and welt on the last 2.5 cm (1in) to allow for rolling. Join edges of neckband. If you are sewing garment by hand join shoulders with a flat seam, then complete as above. Do not press. Hand wash only in soap flakes, 30°C. Short spin, ease to shape, dry flat away from direct sunlight.

DESIGNER TIP:
Knitters with some experience may like to adapt the stocking stitch welts and cuffs in the pattern to rib. The garment will look just as good.

SLALOM

Multicoloured star quality that brightens up the ski slopes or the gloomiest winter day.

SLALOM

MACHINE
Chunky 24 st punchcard.

MATERIALS
Rowan Yarns Aran 100 gm hanks.
C   600(700:700:800) gm Natural
    or Black No: 62
D   100 gm Red No:114
E   100 gm Yellow No:113
F   100 gm Green No:112
G   100 gm Blue No:111
    Small amount of fine yarn in
    background colour.
    2 buttons.

TENSION
Main Tension Dial approx No: 5
18 sts and 23 rows – 10 cm (4in)
square, measured over pattern.

MEASUREMENTS
To fit bust:
    71–76(81–86.5:91.5–
    96.5:101.5–106.5) cm
    28–30(32–34:36–38:40–42) in
Actual size:
    91.5(101.5:112:122) cm
    36(40:44:48) in
Length:
    61(61:63.5:66) cm
    24(24:25:26) in
Sleeve length with cuff turned back:
    43(43:40.5:40.5) cm
    17(17:16:16) in

ABBREVIATIONS
(see page 7)

NOTES
Photographed garment knitted to
fourth size.
Punch cards illustrated before
starting to knit.
NB: Knit side is right side.

PATTERN 1
With the first colour in feeder 1/A
and the second colour in feeder
2/B, K 19 rows C/D.

PATTERN 2
With the first colour in feeder 1/A
and the second colour in feeder
2/B, K as follows: 8 rows C/G, 1
row C/F, 8 rows C/E, 2 rows C/-,

* 8 rows C/D, 2 rows C/-, 2 rows
C/G, 3 rows C/E, 4 rows C/D, 3
rows C/F, 1 row E/F, 3 rows C/E, 4
rows C/G, 2 rows C/-, 8 rows C/D,
2 rows C/-, 8 rows C/F, 1 row C/E,
8 rows C/F *, 2 rows C/-, 26 rows
C/G.

BACK
Lock card 1 on row 1.
NB: Mark each end of row 60.
Push 79(89:99:107) ndls to WP. Set
machine for K1 P1 rib. With D, cast
on selvedge. TD MT -3 RC 000.
Change to C, rib 6 rows. At opp
side to carr push the first
13(17:21:23) sts to HP. Remove the
next 20 sts from machine on WY.
Push the next 13(15:17:21) sts to
HP and remove the next 20 sts
from machine on WY.
    Set carr for partial knitting,
hanging weights under the sts
nearest carr. Rib 23 rows. Rib a
few rows with WY and remove from
machine. Push the next
13(15:17:21) sts to WP, rehang
weights, rib 23 rows, rib a few rows
with WY and remove from
machine. Push rem 13(17:21:23)
sts to WP, rehang weights, rib 23
rows, rib a few rows with WY and
remove from machine. Replace the
20 sts on WY from R of centre on to
machine, over the centre 20 ndls.
** TD MT -1 RC 000. With C, K 1
row, setting machine for patt.
Unlock card and K in pattern 1,
using the fine yarn as follows: On
R, loop the fine yarn over the last st
in D and the outer st adjacent to it
in C. Take the yarn backwards and
forwards each row, always looping
it over the last st in D and the
adjacent C st. Rep on L with a
separate piece of fine yarn. This
prevents laddering, by 'tying' in the
2 sts together. Cont to RC 20.
Remove from machine on WY **.
    Reverse card, locked on row 1.
Replace on machine the rem 20 sts
on WY, over the centre 20 ndls.
Rep from ** to **. Place all sts on
main bed, inc 1 st on L to centre
work. Lock in card 2 on row 1. TD
MT RC 000. With C, K 2 rows,
setting machine for patt on last
row. Unlock card, K as pattern 2 to
RC 108. Lock card, with C cont to
RC 110(110:114:118). K a few

rows with WY and remove from
machine.

FRONT
Work as back to RC 82(82:88:92).
    SHAPE NECK: Slip centre 6 sts
and all sts on opp side to carr on to
WY and remove from machine.
Card row 81(81:87:91). On first
side cont to RC 97(97:103:107).
(Carr centre.) Cast off 3 sts beg
next row and foll alt row, then dec
1 st at neck edge on every alt row
2(2:3:3) times in all, locking card at
RC 108. 8(8:9:9) sts dec in all. With
C, cont straight to RC
110(110:114:118). K a few rows
with WY and remove from
machine.
    Replace rem sts on to machine
over the same ndls as before.
Reset card and ndls (see manual).
With carr at centre, cast off the
first 6 sts, unlock card and
work to match first side of neck.
Remove sts from machine on WY.
Join Shoulders: With W/S of back
facing, place the last row on to
machine, discarding WY. With R/S
of front facing, place front shoulder
sts on top of back sts, leaving
22(22:24:24) sts in centre. Discard
WY. TD 10. With C, K 1 row.
    Cast off.

SLEEVES
Lock card 2 on row 20.
Push 44(48:52:56) ndls to WP.
With WY, cast on and K a few rows.
Change to C. TD MT RC 000.
Shape sides by inc 1 st each end of
5th(5th:10th:14th) and every foll
5th(5th:4th:4th) row 14(15:16:17)
times and AT THE SAME TIME work
in patt as follows: With C, K
10(10:7:7) rows, setting machine
for patt on last row. Unlock card
and work from * to * on pattern 2.
Lock card. With C, K 11(11:8:8)
rows. RC 80(80:74:74). 72(78:84:
90) sts (see note). Cast off.

CUFFS
Lock card 2 on row 81.
Push 33(35:39:41) ndls to WP. Set
machine for K1 P1 rib. With D, cast
on selvedge. Change to C. TD MT -3
RC 000. K 6 rows. Hook up to main

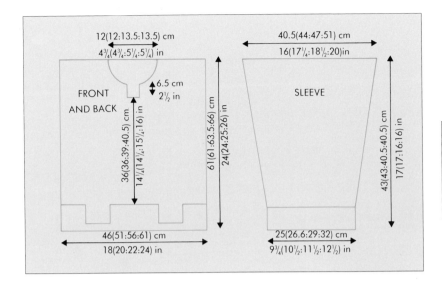

bed, inc 1 st on second and fourth sizes. 33(36:39:42) sts. TD MT RC 000. With C, K 3 rows, setting machine for patt on last row. Unlock card. With C in feeder 1/A and D in feeder 2/B, K 6 rows. Lock card. Break off D. K 3 rows. TD 10 K 1 row. TD MT K 18 rows. With W/S sleeve facing, place first row onto cuff sts as follows: Place 1 st on first ndl, [2 sts on next ndl, 1 st on each of the next 2 ndls] along row. K 1 row loosely by hand.

 Cast off.

BUTTON BAND

Push 9 ndls to WP. Set machine for K1 P1 rib. With C, cast on selvedge. TD MT -3 K 16 rows. Cast off. Buttonhole Band: Work as button band but make a 2 st buttonhole (see note and manual) on 3rd and 12th rows.

COLLAR

Lock card 2 on row 81. Push 71(71:75:75) ndls to WP. Set machine for K1 P1 rib. With D, cast on selvedge. Change to C. TD MT -2 RC 000. K 6 rows. Slip the first and last 4 sts onto pins. Hook up to main bed. TD MT RC 000. K 3 rows, setting machine for patt on last row. With C in feeder 1/A and D in feeder 2/B, unlock card, K 6 rows. Lock card. Break off D. K 7 rows. Cast off. Take the 4 sts on pin and place on to machine as rib sts. TD MT -2. K 18 rows. Cast off.

 Rep with rem 4 sts.

MAKING UP

Sew button bands on to neck opening with cast on edge at top. Sew the 4 rib sts on to collar. Sew collar around neckline, over 5 sts on each of the button bands. Sew on buttons. Join sleeves on to body on machine, or sew in between the markers. Sew sleeve and side seams, turning seam at loose row on cuff. Sew edges of reindeer panels on to welt. Press with a damp cloth all the seams, then the whole garment. Hand wash only in soap flakes, 30°C. Short spin, ease to shape, dry flat away from direct sunlight.

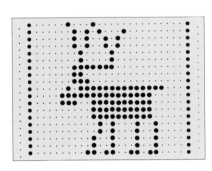

CARD 1

DESIGNER TIP: When the rib is completed, leave the slightly weighted comb on your work to facilitate the knitting of the body of the garment.

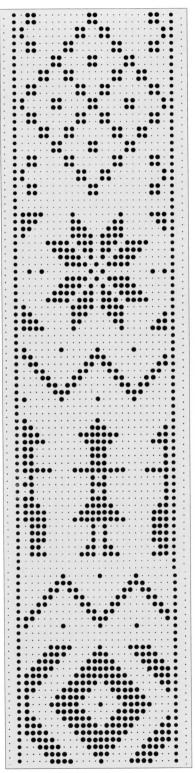

CARD 2

SNOWFLAKES

Defy the winter freezes with confidence in this boldly patterned sweater.

SNOWFLAKES

MACHINE
Chunky 24 st punchcard.

MATERIALS
Hayfield Brig Aran. 50 gm balls.
SWEATER:
MC 13(14:14:15) balls
    No: 028 004
D 8(8:8:9) balls No: 028 001
    Toggle.
MITTS
MC 2 balls No: 028004

TENSION
SWEATER
Main Tension Dial approx No: 5
19 sts and 23 rows – 10 cm (4 in)
square, measured over pattern.
MITTS
Main Tension Dial approx No: 4
18 sts and 28 rows – 10 cm (4 in)
square, measured over st.st.

MEASUREMENTS
To fit bust:
    81–86.5(91.5–96.5:101.5–
    106.5) cm
    32–34(36–38:40–42) in
Actual size:
    101.5(112:122) cm
    40(44:48) in
Length:
    61 cm
    24 in
Sleeve length:
    46 cm
    18 in

ABBREVIATIONS
(see page 7)

NOTES
Photographed garment knitted to
third size.
NB: Knit side is right side.
Punch card illustrated before
starting to knit.

BACK
Lock card on row 1.
NB: Mark each end of row
68(66:64).
Push 95(103:111) ndls to WP. Set
machine for K1 P1 rib. With MC,
cast on selvedge. TD MT -3 RC 000.
Rib 8 rows. Hook up to main bed
inc 1 st on first and second sizes on
L and on third size inc 1 st on L, and
2 sts on R to centre work,
96(104:114) sts. TD MT. K 1 row,
setting machine for patt. Unlock
card. RC 000. With MC in feeder
1/A, and D in feeder 2/B, K as
follows: 2 rows MC/-, 1 row -/D, 2
rows MC/-, 13 rows MC/D, 2 rows
MC/-, 1 row -/D, 1 row MC/-, 73
rows MC/D, 1 row MC/-, 1 row -/D,
2 rows MC/-, 13 rows MC/D, 2
rows MC/-, 1 row -/D. Lock card.
RC 115. Break off D.
    With MC, K 6 rows.
    SHAPE SHOULDERS: (see note).
Cast off 6(7:8) sts beg next 4 rows,
7(7:8) sts beg next 2 rows, 7(8:8) sts
beg next 2 rows and 7(8:9) sts beg
next 2 rows.
    Cast off rem 30(30:32) sts.

FRONT
Work as back to RC 116.
    SHAPE NECK: (see note). Push
centre 8(8:10) sts and all rem sts on
opp side to carr to HP. Set carr for
partial knitting. K 1 row, putting
yarn under first st in HP. K 2 rows.
Cast off 3 sts beg next row and foll
alt row.
    SHAPE SHOULDER: Cont with
neck shaping, cast off 6(7:8) sts
beg next row, 2 sts beg next row.
Cast off the foll sts at beg of the
next 6 rows: 6(7:8), 1, 7(7:8), 1,
7(8:8), 1, Cast off the rem 7(8:9) sts.
Leaving the centre 8(8:10) sts in
HP, push rem sts to WP and work
as for first side. With a spare piece
of MC, cast off the centre sts.

COLLAR
Push 107 ndls to WP. Set machine
for K1 P1 rib. With MC, cast on
selvedge. TD MT -3 RC 000. Rib 50
rows. Cast off.

SLEEVES
Lock card on row 1. Push 56(58:62)
ndls to WP. K a few rows with WY.
Change to MC. TD MT K 1 row,
setting machine for patt. RC 000.
Unlock card. Work in patt as back,
shaping sides by inc 1 st each end
of 15th(10th:5th) row and every foll
5th row to RC 58. Turn card on to
Row 83, cont to inc as set to
86(90:96) sts and RC 91. Lock card.
K 3 rows with MC (see note).
    Cast off.

CUFFS
Push 41(41:45) ndls to WP. Set
machine for K1 P1 rib. With MC,
cast on selvedge. TD MT -3 Rib 10
rows. Hook up to main bed. With
W/S sleeve facing, place sts on WY
on top of cuff as follows: First size:
[Place 2 sts on first ndl, 1 st on each
of the next 2 ndls] to last 2 ndls,
placing 2 sts on each. Second size:
Work as first size to last ndl, place
2 sts on last ndl. Third size: Place 2
sts on each of the first 2 ndls, [Place
1 st on each of the next 2 ndls, and
2 sts on next ndl] to last 2 ndls,
place 2 sts on each of the last 2
ndls. Cast off.

MAKING UP
If you have joined shoulder seams
and sleeves to front and back on
machine continue as follows. Sew
sleeve and side seams. Sew cast off
edge of collar on to neckline
overlapping at the front by 4 cm
(1½ in). Fold in half to the inside and
catch down along neckline. Sew up
sides. Attach toggle 4 cm (1½ in)
from the fold, through both sides of
collar. If you are sewing garment
by hand, join shoulders with a flat
seam. Sew in sleeves to the
markers, then work as given above.
Press according to the instructions
on the ball band and keep one ball
band for washing instructions.

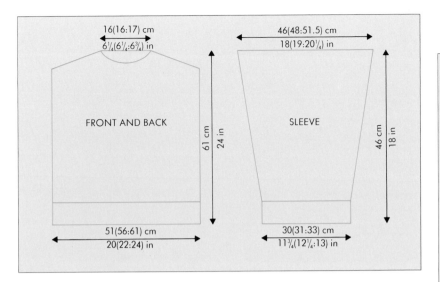

MITTS

Push 33 ndls to WP. Set machine for K1 P1 rib. Cast on selvedge. TD MT -2 RC 000. Rib 18 rows. Hook up to main bed, inc 1 st each end of row. TD MT RC 000. K 10 rows. Leave the first 15 sts nearest carr in WP. Slip next 5 sts on to a pin. Take rem sts off machine on WY. Push empty ndls to NWP. K 8 rows on the first 15 sts, inc 1 st on inner edge on 1st, 3rd and 5th rows. Take these sts off machine on WY. Break off yarn. Take carr across to the other side. Place the 15 sts nearest carr on WY on to machine. Reset RC at 10. Work to match the first 15 sts, inc on inner edge on 1st, 3rd and 5th rows. Replace the first 18 sts on WY on to the machine adjacent to ndls in WP. K 24 rows. Leave the 18 sts nearest carr in WP push the rem 18 sts to HP. Set carr for partial knitting. * With 3 prong tool, work fully fashioned shaping by dec 1 st each end of next and foll alt rows 5 times in all. Cast off. * Push rem 18 sts to WP Reset RC to 42. Work from * to *.

THUMB: Place the 5 sts on pin on to machine, inc 1 st each end of next row, K 1 row. Rep last 2 rows 3 times more (13 sts). K 14 rows. Break off yarn and thread through one eye of double-ended transfer tool. With the other end, take sts off ndls on to tool. Pull yarn through and draw up. Fasten off. Make another mitt the same.

MAKING UP

Sew thumb shaping to main part of mitt. Sew up thumb. Sew edges and top.

DESIGNER TIP:
You can extend the welt if you prefer to make a snug-fitting garment. Allow an extra ball of yarn if you do decide to.

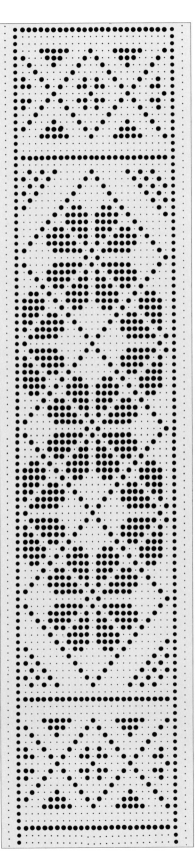

CHAMPAGNE

Casual glamour is the height of luxury in this simple, stunning evening top.

CHAMPAGNE

MACHINE
Chunky.

MATERIALS
Pingouin Feerique and Cotton
Mousse. 50 gm balls and Suedine
40 m (44 yd) hanks.
MC   6(7) balls Feerique No: 01
D   3(4) balls Cotton Mousse
        No: 06
E   3 hanks Suedine No: 02

TENSION
Main Tension Dial approx No: 4
16 sts and 26 rows – 10 cm (4 in)
square, measured over st.st. in
Feerique.

MEASUREMENTS
To fit bust:
    86.5–91.5(96.5–101.5) cm
    34–36(38–40) in
Actual size:
    101.5(112) cm
    40(44) in
Length:
    58.5(63.5) cm
    23(25) in
Sleeve length:
    33(35.5) cm
    13(14) in

ABBREVIATIONS
(see page 7)

NOTES
Photographed garment knitted to
first size.
NB: Purl side is right side

BACK
Push 40(44) ndls to WP. With MC,
cast on with 'e' wrap method.
*** Carr R. TD MT RC 000. Set carr
for partial knitting. * K 1 row. Push
the st nearest carr to HP, K 1 row *.
Rep from * to * to RC 22 (11 sts in
HP). Change to E, rep from * to * to
RC 26. (13 sts in HP). Change to D,
rep from * to * to RC 52. (26 sts in
HP). Change to MC, rep from * to *
to RC 78(86). 1 st remains in WP.
** With MC, push the st nearest
carr in HP to WP, K 2 rows **. Rep
from ** to ** to RC 104(120).
14(18) sts in WP. Change to E, rep
from ** to ** twice to RC 108(124).
16(20) sts in WP. Change to D, rep
from ** to ** to RC 130(146), 13 sts
in HP. Change to E, rep from ** to
** twice to RC 134(150), 11 sts in
HP. Change to MC, rep from ** to
** to RC 156(172)***. Rep from ***
to *** three times more. Cast off.

FRONT
Work as back.

WELT
Push 85(91) ndls to WP. Set
machine for K1 P1 rib. With MC,
cast on selvedge. TD MT –3. RC
000. Rib 24 rows. Hook up to main
bed. With K/S of back facing, take
the opp edge to open side and
place a loop from the row-ends of
this edge evenly on to the rib sts.
Cast off. Rep on front.

SLEEVES
Right front half: Push 40(44) ndls to
WP. With MC, cast on with 'e' wrap
method. Work from *** to *** on
back. K several rows with WY and
remove from machine. Left back
half: Work the same as right front
half. Right back half: Push 40(44)
ndls to WP, cast on with WY, K a
few rows. Change to MC, work
from *** to *** on back. Cast off.
Left front half: Work the same as
Right back half.

CUFFS
Push 49(53) ndls to WP. Set
machine for K1 P1 rib. With MC,
cast on selvedge. TD MT –3 RC
000. Rib 18 rows. Hook up to main
bed. Join two halves of sleeves
together along top seam. With K/S
of sleeve facing, place the sts on
WY on to the cuff sts as follows: First
size: [1 st on first ndl and 2 sts on
each of the foll 2 ndls] along row.
Cast off. Second size: when 3 sts
remain put 1 st on next ndl and
2 sts on last ndl. Cast off.

NECKBAND
(2 pieces alike)
Push 55(61) ndls to WP. Set
machine for K1 P1 rib. With MC,
cast on selvedge. TD MT– 3 RC
000. Rib 6 rows. Hook up to main
bed. Cast off.

MAKING UP
Join shoulder seams. Join cast on
and cast off edges to 15 sts up
from centre front. Rep on back. Sew
cast off edge of neckband on to
front and back. Rep on other side.
Mitre the bottom of the vee by
turning the band inwards to make
a triangle and sew down. Then sew
up centre on neckband. Sew
sleeves on to the front and back,
matching yarns, sew sleeve and
side seams. Press according to the
instructions on the ball bands,
omitting the suedine. Keep ball
bands for washing instructions.

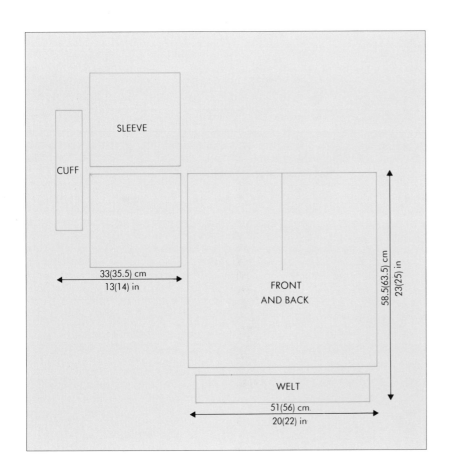

SLEEVE

CUFF

33(35.5) cm
13(14) in

FRONT
AND BACK

58.5(63.5) cm
23(25) in

WELT

51(56) cm.
20(22) in

DESIGNER TIP:
Sew up the seams of this
garment with invisible
thread for a
professional finish.

ENTRELAC

Chase the blues away with the show-stopping colours of this jazzy sweater in softest mohair.

ENTRELAC

MACHINE
Chunky.

MATERIALS
Argyll Finesse. 50 gm balls.
C   4 balls No: 135
E   4 balls No: 136
D   3 balls No: 178
F   3 balls No: 138
     Teazel brush.

TENSION
Main Tension Dial approx No: 3
16 sts and 21 rows – 10 cm (4 in)
square, measured over pattern.

MEASUREMENTS
One size to fit bust:
     86.5 – 101.5 cm
     34 – 40 in
Actual size:
     122 cm
     48 in
Length:
     68.5 cm
     27 in
Sleeve length when cuff rolled:
     47 cm
     18½ in

ABBREVIATIONS
(see page 7)

NOTE
NB: Knit side is right side.

BACK
Welt knitted when back completed.
Push 72 ndls to WP. With C, cast on
using 'e' wrap method. Carr R. TD
MT K 1 row. Push all sts to HP,
except the st nearest the carr. Set
carr for partial knitting.
     FOUNDATION TRIANGLES: * RC
000. K 2 rows. [Push the next st in
HP to WP. K 2 rows] until 11 sts in
WP. Push one more st to WP, K 1
row RC 23. (Yarn is nearest the sts
in HP). Push the 12 sts in WP to HP.
Push the carr across to L *. Push the
13th st to WP, hang a small claw
weight on to sts in WP, rep from * to
* 5 times more, but do not push the
carr across to L after last rep. 6
base triangles worked.
     FIRST ROW OF BLOCKS: End

Triangle: Change to E. RC 000.
Move first st on R on to adjacent
empty ndl. Place empty ndl in
NWP. K 2 rows. ** Inc 1 st on R and
move the first st in HP (nearest carr)
on to the st in WP. Place empty ndl
in NWP. K 2 rows **. (RC 4, 2 sts in
WP, 2 empty ndls between sts in
HP and WP). Rep from ** to ** once.
     Using 3 prong tool move the
rem sts from the first base triangle
along on to the 3 empty ndls, so
there are still 9 sts in HP, but the
strain has been taken off the yarn.
Cont to rep from ** to **, always
moving along the sts when there
are 3 empty ndls between HP and
WP sts. Cont to RC 23. (12 sts in
WP in E). 12 empty ndls between
sts in HP and sts in WP. Push the 12
sts in WP to HP. Push carr to R.
     First Block: *** RC 000. Pick up
12 sts from the row-ends of the
foundation triangle, placing them
on to the 12 empty ndls. K 2 rows
over these 12 sts. Remembering to
move along the sts with transfer
tool, to prevent straining the yarn,
[transfer the first st in HP from
adjacent triangle on L on to the
adjacent st in WP. Push empty ndl
to NWP. K 2 rows] 11 times, RC 24.
Transfer last st in HP on to adjacent
st in WP, K 1 row. RC 25. There are
12 empty ndls and 12 sts in WP.
Push these 12 sts to HP. Push carr
to R ***. Rep from *** to *** 4 times
more. 5 blocks worked.
     End Triangle: Pick up 12 sts from
the row-ends of the last foundation
triangle. K 2 rows. [Dec 1 st on L, K
2 rows] until 1 st remains. RC 23.
Move this rem st over to L and
place on 12th ndl. (11 empty ndls,
between this and ndls in HP.) This
completes the first row of blocks.
     SECOND ROW OF BLOCKS:
First Block: On to the 11 empty ndls,
place 11 sts from the row-ends of
the end triangle. **** RC 000. With
F, K 2 rows. Place the first st in HP
onto the adjacent st in WP. Push
empty ndl to NWP. With D, K 2
rows. Push the first st in HP on to the
adjacent st in WP. Push the empty
ndl to NWP. With F, K 2 rows. Rep
last 4 rows, moving along the sts in
HP to prevent strain on yarn, as
before. Cont to RC 25, 12 empty
ndls. Push 12 sts in WP to HP. Push
carr to L.

Second Block: Pick up 12 sts
from row-ends of next block and
place on to ndls ****. Work from
**** to **** once, then work from
**** to **** twice using only D.
Work from **** to **** twice as the
first block in 2 row stripes of F and
D. This completes second row of
blocks.
     THIRD ROW OF BLOCKS: Work
as first row of blocks using C
instead of E.
     FOURTH ROW OF BLOCKS:
Work as second row of blocks, in
colours as follows: First, Second,
Fifth and Sixth blocks in E. Third
and Fourth blocks work in 2 row
stripes of F and E.
     FIFTH ROW OF BLOCKS: Work
as third row of blocks.
     SIXTH ROW OF BLOCKS: Work
as second row of blocks.
     SEVENTH ROW OF BLOCKS:
Work as first row of blocks.
     FINISHING TRIANGLES: Carr L.
***** Pick up 11 sts on to the 11
empty ndls from the row-ends of
the last triangle. With C, [K 2 rows.
Place first st in HP on to the
adjacent st in WP, dec 1 st on L]
until 1 st remains in WP. Transfer
last st in HP on to st on L. K 2 rows.
One st remains, replace this st on to
12th ndl, leaving 11 empty ndls
between this st and ndls in HP *****.
Work from ***** to ***** making 6
finishing triangles in all.
     Cast off last st.

YOKE
Push 96 ndls to WP. With W/S of
work facing, place 16 loops from
each of the finishing triangles on to
ndls. TD MT RC 000. K 4 rows F, 2
rows E, 4 rows F, 2 rows D, 4 rows
F, 2 rows E, 4 rows F, 2 rows D, 4
rows F, 2 rows E, 4 rows F. RC 34. K
several rows with WY across all the
sts and remove from machine.

FRONT
Work as back to Yoke.

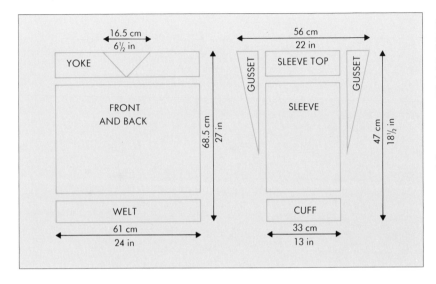

CUFFS
Push 36 ndls to WP. TD MT –1. With W/S sleeve facing, place 12 loops from each of the foundation triangles. K as follows: [4 rows F, 2 rows D, 4 rows F, 2 rows E] twice, then K 4 rows F, 2 rows D and 6 rows F. Cast off.

GUSSET
With C, cast on 2 sts with 'e' wrap method. TD MT RC 000. Keeping one side straight, inc 1 st on other side on 3rd and every foll 3rd row to 23 sts. RC 66. Cast off. Make one more the same. Make two more reversing shaping.

MAKING UP
Join centre back seam on collar. Overlap collar at front and catch down row-ends on outside and inside. Sew straight edge of gusset on to sleeve, so that widest part of gusset is at the top of the sleeve. With a second gusset rep on the other side of sleeve. Sew sleeve and wide end of gusset on to front and back, to its full depth. Sew sleeve and side seams. Brush all over with a teazel brush. Do not press, but keep one ball band for washing instructions.

YOKE
Push 48 ndls to WP. With W/S of work facing place 16 loops from each of the first three finishing triangles on R on to ndls. Work in the same colour sequence as back yoke, shaping V neck by dec 1 st on L on second and every foll alt row 13 times in all. Cont straight to RC 34. K several rows with WY and remove from machine. Work the other side of the yoke to match reversing shaping, leaving the shoulder sts on the machine. Replace the shoulder sts on WY on to the machine, leaving 26 empty ndls between shoulder sts. With R/S back facing place the 96 back sts on WY on top of front sts, with the back neck sts on the 26 empty ndls. Cast off loosely.

COLLAR
Right Side: Push 37 ndls to WP. With W/S of R/S of front and back facing, place the edge of the V neck on to 24 ndls and place 13 sts to centre back neck on the rem ndls. TD MT RC 000. K 4 rows E, 2 rows D, 4 rows E, 2 rows C, 4 rows E, 2 rows D and 4 rows E. Cast off. Left Side: Work as right side of neck, in the following colour sequence: K 4 rows D, 2 rows C, 4 rows D, 2 rows E, 4 rows D, 2 rows C and 4 rows D. Cast off.

WELT
(Back and front alike)
Push 78 ndls to WP. With W/S work facing, pick up 13 loops from each foundation triangle and place on ndls. TD MT –1 RC 000. [K 4 rows F, 2 rows D, 4 rows F, 2 rows E] 3 times, then K 6 rows F. Cast off.

SLEEVES
Push 36 ndls to WP. Work as given for back, making three base triangles. Work in the same method as back:
FIRST AND FIFTH ROW OF BLOCKS: K with E.
SECOND AND FOURTH ROW OF BLOCKS: First and Third blocks in 2 row stripes of F and D. Second block in D.
THIRD ROW OF BLOCKS: As First row of block using C.
FINISHING TRIANGLES: Work as back.

SLEEVE TOP
Push 54 ndls to WP. With W/S sleeve facing, pick up 18 loops from each of the finishing triangles onto ndls. TD MT K as follows: 4 rows F, 2 rows E, 4 rows F, 2 rows D, 4 rows F. Cast off.

DESIGNER TIP:
All completed mohair garments should be brushed vigorously with a teazel brush to release the pile of the yarn. The end result will be spectacular compared with the appearance of the knitting when it has just come off the machine.

GREY
FLANNEL

Suit yourself in this simply elegant two-piece, knitted in a muted feminine grey.

GREY FLANNEL

MACHINE
Standard Gauge.

SWEATER

MATERIALS
Sirdar Country Style 4 ply. 50 gm balls.
 7(8:8:8:8) balls No: 408.
 3 buttons, 1 press stud.

TENSION
Main Tension Dial approx No: 7
28 sts and 44 rows – 10 cm (4 in) square, measured over st.st.

MEASUREMENTS
To fit bust:
 81–86.5(91.5–96.5:101.5–
 106.5:112–117) cm
 32–34(36–38:40–42:44–46) in
Actual size:
 91.5(101.5:112:122) cm
 36(40:44:48) in
Length:
 61(63.5:66:68.5) cm
 24(25:26:27) in
Sleeve length:
 43(44.5:46:47) cm
 17(17½:18:18½) in

ABBREVIATIONS
(see page 7)

NOTES
Photographed garment knitted to third size.
NB: Knit side is right side.

BACK
Push 129(143:157:171) ndls to WP. Set machine for K1 P1 rib. Cast on selvedge. TD MT -4 RC 000. Rib 40 rows. Hook up to main bed, inc 1 st on L to centre work. TD MT RC 000. K to RC 116(120:126:130).
 SHAPE ARMHOLE: Dec 1 st beg next 20 rows. (10 sts dec each side). RC 136(140:146:150). Cont to RC 222(230:242:250).
 SHAPE SHOULDERS: (see note). Cast off 7(8:10:11) sts beg next 4 rows, 7(9:10:11) sts beg next 4 rows, 8(9:10:13) sts beg next 2 rows. Cast off rem 38 sts.

FRONT
Work as back to RC 170(178:190:198). Place centre 10 sts and all rem sts on opp side to carr on to WY and remove from machine. Push empty ndls to NWP. K on first side of front to RC 213(221:233:241). Carr centre.
 SHAPE NECK: (see note). Cast off 5 sts beg next row and the foll sts on every alt row: 3, 3, 2, 1. Cont to RC 222(230:242:250).
 SHAPE SHOULDER: Cast off 7(8:10:11) sts beg next row and foll alt row. K 1 row. Cast off 7(9:10:11) sts beg next and foll alt row. K 1 row. Cast off rem 8(9:10:13) sts. Replace rem front on machine, discarding WY. Carr centre. Reset RC 213(221:233:241). Cast off the first 10 sts, cont to match first side, reversing shaping.

SLEEVES
Push 78(82:90:94) ndls to WP. K a few rows with WY. Change to MC. TD MT RC 000. Shape sides by inc 1 st each end of 2nd and every foll 4th row to 140(146:154:158) sts. RC 120(124:130:136).
 SHAPE ARMHOLE: Dec 1 st beg next 20 rows (see note).
 Cast off.

CUFFS
Push 59(61:67:71) ndls to WP. Set machine for K1 P1 rib. Cast on selvedge. TD MT -4 RC 000. Rib 36 rows. Hook up to main bed. With W/S of sleeve facing, place the first row on top of the cuff sts as follows: First and Fourth sizes: [Place 1 st on each of the first 2 ndls and 2 sts on next ndl] along row. Second and Third sizes: [Place 2 sts on first ndl, place 1 st on each of the next 2 ndls] to last ndl, place 2 sts on last ndl. K 1 row loosely by hand.
 Cast off.

BUTTON BAND
Push 19 ndls to WP. Set machine for K1 P1 rib. Cast on selvedge. TD MT -4 RC 000. Rib 54 rows. Cast off. Buttonhole Band: Work as button band making a 2 st buttonhole (see note and manual) on RC 4, 27 and 50. Rib 4 rows. Cast off.

COLLAR
Push 131 ndls to WP. Set machine for K1 P1 rib. Cast on selvedge. TD MT RC 000. Rib 38 rows. Cast off.

MAKING UP
If you have joined shoulders and sleeves on the machine, then sew on front bands. Sew on cast off edge of collar around neckline, over half of the band sts each side. Sew sleeve and side seams. If you are sewing garment by hand, join the shoulder seams with a flat seam, sew in sleeves, matching shaping. Continue to make up as given above. Press according to instructions on the ball band. Sew on buttons. Sew press stud on edge of band. Keep one ball band for washing instructions.

SKIRT

MATERIALS
Sirdar Country Style 4 ply. 50 gm balls.
 8(9:9) balls No: 408.
 2.5 cm wide elastic for top band.

MEASUREMENTS
To fit hips:
 86.5–91.5(91.5–96.5:96.5–
 101.5) cm
 34–36(36–38:38–40) in
Actual size:
 91.5(96.5:101.5) cm
 36(38:40) in
Length:
 Including waistband:
 76 cm
 30 in

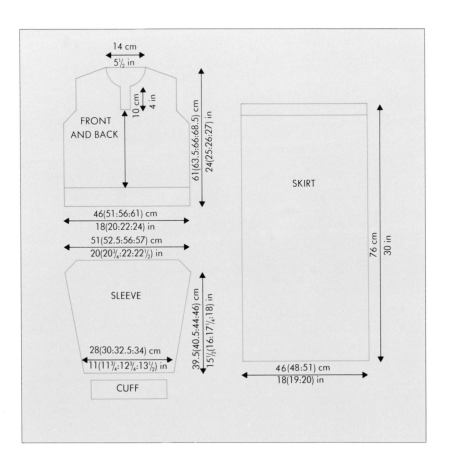

14 cm
5½ in

10 cm
4 in

FRONT
AND BACK

61(63.5:66:68.5) cm
24(25:26:27) in

46(51:56:61) cm
18(20:22:24) in

51(52.5:56:57) cm
20(20¾:22:22½) in

SLEEVE

39.5(40.5:44:46) cm
15½(16:17¼:18) in

28(30:32.5:34) cm
11(11¾:12¾:13½) in

CUFF

SKIRT

76 cm
30 in

46(48:51) cm
18(19:20) in

TENSION
Main Tension Dial approx No: 5
33 sts and 74 rows – 10 cm (4in)
square, measured over Fishermans
Rib.

BACK
Push 151(159:167) ndls to WP. Set
machine for K1 P1 rib. Cast on
selvedge. TD MT. Set carr for
Fishermans Rib (see manual). RC
000. Rib 540 rows. Set carr for K1
P1 rib. TD MT -1. Rib 30 rows.
Hook up to main bed. Pick up a
loop from the first K1 P1 row on to
the first st. Rep along row to make
a hem. Cast off.
    Work the front the same.

MAKING UP
Join side seams and one side of
hem. Thread elastic through hem.
Join ends. Sew up side of hem.
Keep one ball band for washing
instructions.

DESIGNER TIP:
**Man-made fibres should
always be pressed with
great care and attention
to the manufacturer's
recommendations.**

CHECKMATE

A winner every time – jewel colours strategically placed on black for maximum playing power.

CHECKMATE

MACHINE
Standard Gauge 24 st punchcard.

MATERIALS
Rowan Yarns Lightweight DK. 500 gm cones.

C 1(1:2) cones No: 61
D 1 cone No: 129
E 1 cone No: 2
F 1 cone No: 12
G 1 cone No: 90
H 1 cone No: 43
I 1 cone No: 501
   4 Buttons.

TENSION
Main Tension Dial approx No: 10
29 sts and 32 rows – 10 cm (4 in) square, measured over pattern.

MEASUREMENTS
To fit bust:
    91.5(101.5:112) cm
    36(40:44) in
Actual size:
    106.5(117:127) cm
    42(46:50) in
Length:
    63.5(63.5:66) cm
    25(25:26) in
Sleeve length:
    40.5(40.5:43) cm
    16(16:17) in

ABBREVIATIONS
(see page 7)

NOTES
Photographed garment knitted to third size.
NB: Knit side is right side.
Punch card illustrated before starting to knit.

POCKET LINING
(make 2)
Push 60 ndls to WP. With C, cast on with 'e' wrap method. TD MT. K 43 rows. K a few rows with WY and remove from machine.

RIGHT FRONT AND RIGHT BACK
Lock card on row 1.
Push 107(125:137) ndls to WP. Set machine for K1 P1 rib. With C, cast on selvedge. TD MT –2 RC 000. Rib 16(16:20) rows. Hook up to main bed, inc 1 st on L to centre work. TD MT RC 000. K 1 row, setting carr for patt. Unlock card. With the first colour in feeder 1/A and the second colour in feeder 2/B, K as follows: 12 rows C/E, 6 rows D/F, 6 rows D/I, 6 rows G/H, 6 rows G/F, 6 rows D/H, 1 row D/- RC 43. Take centre 60 sts off machine on WY and replace with pocket lining sts with W/S facing. Cont in patt: 1 row D/-, 2 rows D/F, 2 rows D/I, 2 rows D/G, 2 rows D/H, 2 rows D/F. RC 54. ** 2 rows C/D, 2 rows C/-, * 2 rows C/E, 2 rows C/-. Rep from * 4 times, 2 rows D/C, 4 rows D/H, 2 rows F/H, 2 rows F/G, 2 rows H/G, 2 rows H/C, 2 rows I/C, 2 rows H/C, 2 rows H/G, 2 rows F/G, 2 rows F/H, 4 rows D/H **. RC 106. On opp side to carr remove all sts from centre 0, on WY, from machine. Card row No: 107. Turn back card to row 55. Reset ndls (see manual) cont on first set of sts. Work from ** to ** RC 158. K 2 rows C/D, 12 rows C/E. Lock card.
  K 1 row C. Set machine for K1 P1 rib. Transfer sts, put in comb and weights. TD MT – 1 RC 000. Rib 16(16:20) rows. Hook up to main bed.
  *** K several rows with WY and remove from machine. Replace sts from second side, on WY, and place on to the same ndls as before. Reset card and ndls. Work to match first side to ***. Place the first set of sts on WY on top of sts on machine. Cast off both sets together.

POCKET TOP
Push 61 ndls to WP. Set machine for K1 P1 rib. With D, cast on selvedge. TD MT –2. Rib 4 rows. Hook up to main bed dec 1 st on L. With W/S of work facing, place the pocket sts on WY on top of rib sts, cast off both sets of sts together.

LEFT FRONT AND LEFT BACK
Work exactly the same as right front and right back.

SLEEVES
Lock card on row 1.
Push 71(81:91) ndls to WP. Set machine for K1 P1 rib. With C, cast on selvedge. TD MT – 3 RC 000. Rib 6(6:10) rows. Hook up to main bed, inc 1 st on L to centre work. TD MT RC 000. K 1 row, setting machine for patt. Unlock card. Shape sides by inc 1 st each end of 20th and every foll 3rd row to 138(148:158) sts and AT THE SAME TIME work in patt as follows: Work as back to RC 106. K 2 rows C/D, 12 rows C/E. Lock card. K 1 row C. Set machine for K1 P1 rib. Transfer sts, insert comb and weights. TD MT –1. Rib 6(6:10) rows. Cast off.

BACK PANEL
Push 79 ndls to WP. Set machine for K1 P1 rib. With C, cast on selvedge. TD MT –3 RC 000. Rib 200(200:210) rows. Cast off.

BUTTON BAND AND COLLAR
Left Side: Push 79 ndls to WP. Set machine for K1 P1 rib. With C, cast on selvedge. TD MT –3 RC 000. Rib 200(200:210) rows. Shape Dart: Set carr for partial knitting, [push 8 sts at opp end to carr to HP, K 2 rows] until 7 sts remain. Rib across all sts. Rib a further 22 rows. Cast off.
  Right Side: Work as left side, making buttonholes as follows: Work to RC 28. Leave the first 7 sts, make a 2 st buttonhole over the next 2 sts (see manual). Rep on opp side of work. Work to RC 68 and

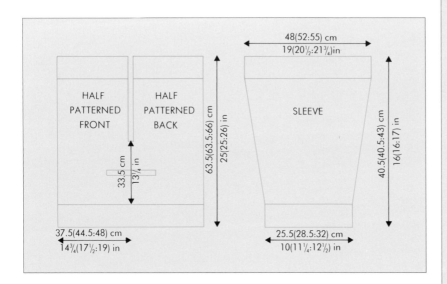

rep buttonhole row. Cont to match left side, reversing shaping.

MAKING UP

Sew ends horizontally into work. Sew down pocket linings and sew edges of pocket tops. Sew back panel on to left and right back. Sew shortest edge of button band and collar on to the front, lining up dart with shoulder seam. Join cast off edges of collar, then sew on to back panel firmly. Sew on buttons, sew sleeves into armholes, then sew sleeve seams. Press with a damp cloth. Hand wash only in soap flakes, 30°C. Short spin, ease to shape, dry flat away from direct sunlight.

DESIGNER TIP:
When sewing on the buttons, make sure that the patterns on either side of the central panel match and are aligned.

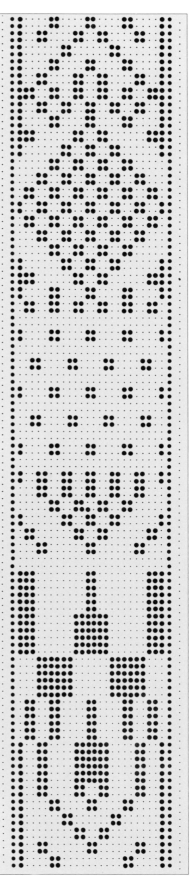

EXECUTIVE

A warm sweater in subtle colour tones for the man about town.

E**X**ECUTIVE

MACHINE
Standard Gauge 24 st punchcard.

MATERIALS
Rowan Yarns Lightweight DK. 500 gm cones.
C 1(1:2:2) cones No: 615
D 1 cone No: 52
E 1 cone No: 6
F 1 cone No: 411

TENSION
Main Tension Dial approx No:10
30 sts and 35 rows – 10 cm (4 in) square, measured over pattern.

MEASUREMENTS
To fit chest:
    91.5(96.5:101.5:106.5) cm
    36(38:40:42) in
Actual size:
    106.5(112:117:122) cm
    42(44:46:48) in
Length:
    63.5(66:68:71) cm
    25(26:27:28) in
Sleeve length:
    43(46:46:48) cm
    17(18:18:19) in

ABBREVIATIONS
(see page 7)

NOTES
Photographed garment knitted to fourth size.
NB: Knit side is right side.
Punch cards illustrated before starting to knit.

PATTERN 1
With the first colour in feeder 1/A and the second colour in feeder 2/B, K as follows: 8 rows F/E, 16 rows C/F, 2 rows D/E, 16 rows C/F. These 42 rows form the patt. 1st size starts after 26 rows of pattern, 2nd size starts after 16 rows of pattern, 3rd size starts after 8 rows of pattern and 4th size starts at beg of pattern. Card row Nos: 27(17:9:1).

PATTERN 2
K rows as given in instructions with C/F.

BACK
Lock card 1 on row 27(17:9:1).
NB: Mark each end of row 100(104:108:112) with WY. Push 161(167:175:181) ndls to WP. Set machine for K1 P1 rib. With C, cast on selvedge. TD MT -3 RC 000. Rib 30 rows. Hook up to main bed, inc 1 st on L to centre work. TD MT RC 000. K 1 row setting carr for patt. Unlock card, K in pattern 1 to RC 166(176:184:192). Replace card 1 with card 2, locked on row 1. (See manual for resetting ndls). Unlock card, K in patt 2 to RC 180(190:198:206).
    SHAPE SHOULDERS: (see note).
Cont in patt, cast off 9(10:11:11) sts beg next 6 rows, 10(10:11:12) sts beg next 2 rows, 10(10:10:11) sts beg next 4 rows. Cast off rem 48 sts.

FRONT
Work as back to RC 166(176:184:192).
    SHAPE NECK: (see note). Push centre 14 sts to HP and all rem sts on opp side to carr. Set carr for partial knitting. With card 2, cont in patt as back, K 1 row, putting yarn under first st in HP. K 2 rows. Cast off 4 sts beg next and foll 2 alt rows, K 1 row, cast off 3 sts beg next row, K 1 row. Cast off 2 sts beg next row (17 sts dec in all). Cont straight to RC 180(190:198:206).
    SHAPE SHOULDER: (see note). Cast off 9(10:11:11) sts beg next and foll 2 alt rows, K 1 row, cast off 10(10:11:12) sts beg next row, K 1 row, cast off 10(10:10:11) sts beg next row, K 1 row, cast off rem 10(10:10:11) sts. Leave centre 14 sts in HP, push all rem sts to WP. Work to match first side. With a spare piece of yarn, cast off the rem 14 sts.

SLEEVES
Lock card 1 on row 17(9:9:1).
Push 74(80:84:90) ndls to WP. With WY, cast on and K a few rows. With C, K 1 row, setting carr for patt. TD MT RC 000. Unlock card, K in pattern 1 to RC 110(118:118:126) while AT THE SAME TIME shaping sides by inc 1 st each end of 3rd and every foll 3rd row 36(37:39:40) times. 146(154:162:170) sts. Replace card 1 with card 2. Unlock card, K in pattern 2 to RC 122(130:130:138). (See note.) Cast off.

CUFFS
Push 55(59:61:63) ndls to WP. Set machine for K1 P1 rib. With C, cast on selvedge. TD MT -3 RC 000. Rib 30 rows. Hook up to main bed. Push out one extra ndl on L on first, second and third sizes. With W/S of sleeve facing, place the sts on WY on to cuff sts as follows. First size: * place 2 sts on first ndl, and 1 st on each of the next 2 ndls *. Rep from * to *, ending with 2 sts on last ndl. Second size: place 1 st on first ndl, then rep from * to * on first size, ending with 1 st on last ndl. Third size: place 2 sts on first ndl, then rep from * to * on first size, ending with 2 sts on last ndl. Fourth size: Place 2 sts on each of the first 4 ndls, then rep from * to * on first size, ending with 2 sts on each of the last 5 ndls. K 1 row loosely by hand. Cast off.

NECKBAND
Push 124 ndls to WP. Set machine for K1 P1 rib. With C, cast on selvedge. TD MT -3 RC 000. Rib 12 rows. Hook up to main bed (see note). Cast off.

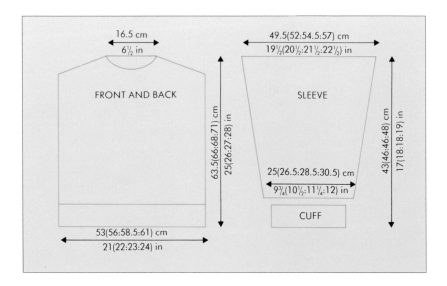

MAKING UP

If you have joined shoulders, neckband and sleeves to body on machine, then sew sleeve and side seams. If sewing garment by hand, then join shoulders with a flat seam, sew in sleeves to the WY markers, sew sleeve and side seams and sew on neckband. Press seams with a damp cloth, then the whole garment. Hand wash only in soap flakes, 30°C. Short spin, ease to shape, dry flat away from direct sunlight.

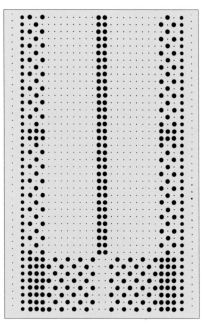

CARD 1

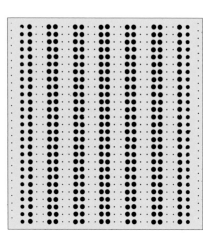

CARD 2

DESIGNER TIP:
When lengthening or shortening the sleeves of a garment with a definite pattern, such as this, you must be careful to do so without disrupting the flow of the design.

VICE VERSA

Create an optical illusion when you wear this striking two-tone dress.

VICE VERSA

MACHINE
Chunky 24 st punchcard.

MATERIALS
Sirdar Wash'n' Wear Aran. 40 gm balls.
E 11(13:15) balls No: 432
F 11(13:15) balls No: 483

TENSION
Main Tension Dial approx No: 4
19 sts and 24 rows – 10 cm (4 in) square, measured over pattern.

MEASUREMENTS
To fit bust:
    81-86.5(91.5-96.5:101.5-106.5) cm
    32-34(36-38:40-42) in
Actual size:
    101.5(112:122) cm
    40(44:48) in
Length:
    101.5(104:106.5) cm
    40(41:42) in
Sleeve seam:
    51 cm
    20 in

ABBREVIATIONS
(see page 7)

NOTES
Photographed garment knitted to third size.
NB: Knit side is right side.
Punch card illustrated before starting to knit.

LEFT FRONT AND LEFT BACK
Lock card on row 1. Push 83(93:103) ndls to WP. Set machine for K1 P1 rib. With E, cast on selvedge. TD MT –2 RC 000. Rib 10 rows. Hook up to main bed, inc 1 st on L to centre work. TD MT. K 1 row setting carr for patt. Unlock card. RC 000. Carr R. With E in feeder 1/A and F in feeder 2/B, work as follows: K to RC 28. Shape sides by inc 1 st each end of next and every foll 12th row 5 times in all. 94(104:114) sts. Cont straight to RC 166(168:170). Card row No: 47(49:51). Place all sts on L from centre 0 on to WY and remove from machine. Push empty ndls to NWP.

Left Front: K1 row.
    SHAPE RAGLAN: * Cast off 7(9:10) sts beg next row, cont to dec 1 st on this edge on foll 9th(7th:5th) row, then every foll 5th row to RC 220(224:230).
    SHAPE NECK: Cont with raglan shaping as set, cast off 4(5:6) sts beg next row, 4 sts on foll alt row, 3 sts on foll alt row and 2 sts on next alt row. K1 row, dec 1 st beg next row. 14(15:16) sts dec in all. Cont to RC 230(236:242). 15(16:18) sts remain, slip on to WY and remove from machine.
    Left Back: Replace sts on to the same ndls as before, reset card to row 47(49:51). Reset ndls (see manual). Carr L. K1 row. Work from * on left front, omitting neck shaping, keeping L/S of work straight, to RC 231(237:243). Carr R. Take the first 15(16:18) sts off machine on WY, K a few rows with WY over the rem 14(15:16) sts and remove from machine. Replace the 15(16:18) sts on machine with R/S facing. Place sts from left front on top. Cast off both sets of sts together.

RIGHT FRONT AND RIGHT BACK
Work as left front and left back, reversing the colours, and neck shaping.

LEFT BACK AND LEFT FRONT NECKBAND
With W/S of work facing, pick up 32(34:36) sts from neckline. TD MT RC 000. Inc 1 st each end of row. With E, K 10 rows. Cast off. Rep on right back and right front, using F instead of E.

LEFT SLEEVE
Lock card on row 35.
Push 50(56:62) ndls to WP. With E, cast on with 'e' wrap method. TD MT RC 000. K 32 (38:44) rows. K1 row, setting machine for patt. Unlock card. RC 000. With E in feeder 1/A and F in feeder 2/B, K in patt, shaping sides by inc 1 st each end of 13th (7th:1st) row and every foll 3rd row 22(24:26) times in all. 94(104:114) sts. RC 76. K 10 rows straight.
    SHAPE TOP: First size: Cast off 4 sts beg next 20 rows. Second size: Cast off 4 sts beg next 10 rows, then 5 sts beg next 10 rows. Third size: Cast off 5 sts beg next 20 rows.
    All sizes: Cast off rem 14 sts.

RIGHT SLEEVE
Work as left sleeve, reversing the colours.

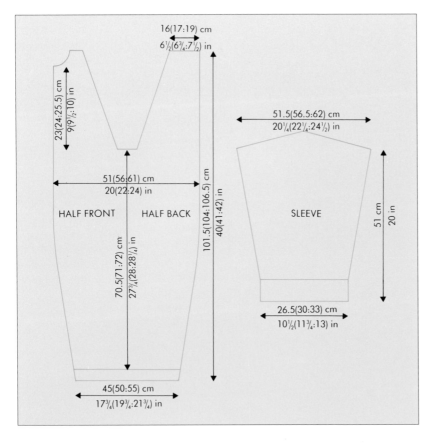

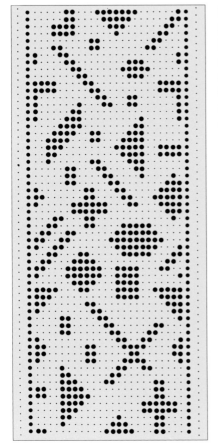

MAKING UP

Sew centre front and centre back seams carefully. Sew raglan seams. Sew straight rows on sleeve, on to the raglan cast off sts. Sew sleeve seam, reversing seam to allow for cuff turn back. Join neckband seams. Press according to instructions on the ball band, and keep one ball band for washing instructions.

SCARF

Push 45 ndls to WP. Set machine for K1 P1 rib. With F, cast on selvedge. TD MT -2 RC 000. Rib 90 rows. Cast off. Push 45 ndls to WP. Set machine for K1 P1 rib. With E, cast on selvedge. TD MT -2 RC 000. Rib 21 rows. Take 23 sts on opp side to carr off machine on WY. On rem sts rib 14 rows. Take these sts off machine on WY. Replace the first 23 sts on WY on to machine, discarding WY. Rib 14 rows. Replace rem sts on WY on to machine. Rib 55 rows. Cast off. Join both cast off edges together.

DESIGNER TIP:
Backstitch the front and back seams with great care to avoid unsightly stitches showing through in the opposite colour on the two halves of the dress.

CREEPY CRAWLIES

A cheerful red sweater festooned with weird and wonderful woollen beasties.

EARL GREY

Masculine tones of grey are highlighted with cherry red in this roomy weekend sweater.

CREEPY CRAWLIES

MACHINE
Standard Gauge 24 st punchcard.

MATERIALS
Patons Diploma 4 ply. 50 gm balls.
4(4:5:5) No: 4732 balls   C
2(2:2:3) No: 4703 balls   D
1 No: 4733 ball   E
1 No: 4736 ball   F

TENSION
Main Tension Dial approx No: 9
30 sts and 36 rows – 10 cm (4 in)
square, measured over pattern.

MEASUREMENTS
To fit chest:
61(66:71:76) cm
24(26:28:30) in
Actual size:
66(71:76:81) cm
26(28:30:32) in
Length:
43(46:48:51) cm
17(18:19:20) in
Sleeve seam:
30.5(35.5:35.5:38) cm
12(14:14:15) in

ABBREVIATIONS
(see page 7)

NOTES
Photographed garment knitted to
third size.
NB: Knit side is right side.
Punch cards illustrated before
starting to knit.

CORDS
With E cast on 6 sts by 'e' wrap
method. K 1 row. TD MT –4. Set
carr for knitting in one direction. K
to RC 38 (19 rows). Slip sts on to a
pin. Make 7 more in E.
Make 10 in F.

BACK
Lock card 1 on row 1.
NB: Mark each end of row
64(72:80:88).
Push 99(107:115:123) ndls to WP.
Set machine for K1 P1 rib. With C,
cast on selvedge. TD MT –2 RC
000. Rib 26 rows. Hook up to main
bed, inc 1 st on L to centre work. TD
MT RC 000. K 1 row, setting
machine for patt. Unlock card. With
C in feeder 1/A and D in feeder
2/B, K to RC 110(120:130:140).
Lock card. Break off D. Cont with C,
K to RC 122(132:142:152).
SHAPE SHOULDERS: (see note).
Cast off 7(8:9:10) sts beg next 4
rows, 8(9:9:10) sts beg next 2 rows,
10(10:11:11) sts beg next 2 rows.
Cast off loosely the rem
36(38:40:42) sts.

FRONT
Work as back to RC 112(122:
132:142).
SHAPE NECK: (see note).
Push the centre 10(12:14:16) sts
and all sts on opp side to carr to
HP. * Set carr for partial knitting. K
1 row, slipping yarn under the first
ndl in HP. K 2 rows. Cast off the foll
sts at beg of next and every foll alt
rows: 4, 3, 3, 2, 1 and AT THE
SAME TIME at RC 122(132:142:
152) shape shoulders by casting off
7(8:9:10) sts beg next row and foll
alt row. K 1 row, cast off 8(9:9:10)
sts beg next row, K 1 row, cast off
rem 10(10:11:11) sts. Leaving
centre 10(12:14:16) sts in HP, push
rem sts to WP. Work to match first
side from *. Cast off centre
10(12:14:16) sts with a spare piece
of C.

SLEEVES
Push 46(52:62:68) ndls to WP. Cast
on with WY. K a few rows. Change
to C. TD MT RC 000. Shape sides
by inc 1 st each end of 7th(5th:
8th:8th) row and every foll
7th(7th:8th:8th) row 15(17:14:16)
times in all. 76(86:90:100) sts and
AT THE SAME TIME work in patt to
RC 110(120:120:130) as follows:
With C, K 8 rows, with D, K 2 rows.
Introduce an 'E' cord as follows: On
R of centre, take st Nos: 11 and 12
off machine on to 2 prong tool,
insert cord between work and
machine, put 3 sts on each of the
empty ndls. Replace the 2 sts on
tool on top.
Cont working 8 rows C, 2 rows
D, inserting cords on the foll ndls:
RC 20. On L of centre, an 'F' cord
on sts 14 and 15. RC 30. On R
of centre an 'F' cord on sts 21 and
22. RC 50. An 'E' cord on centre 2
sts. RC 60. On L of centre, an 'F'
cord on sts 21 and 22. RC 70. On R
of centre an 'E' cord on sts 12 and
13. RC 90. On L of centre an 'F'
cord on sts 9 and 10. RC 110. Only
on the second, third and fourth
sizes: on R of centre an 'F' cord on
sts 18 and 19. On L of centre an 'E'
cord on sts 18 and 19. At RC
110(120:120:130) (see note).
Cast off.

CUFFS
Push 43(49:49:51) ndls to WP. Set
machine for K1 P1 rib. With C, cast
on selvedge. TD MT –2 RC 000. Rib
20 rows, hook up to main bed.
With W/S sleeve facing, place the
first row on top of cuff sts, dec as
follows: First and second sizes:
Place 2 sts on first and last ndls and
2 sts on centre ndl. Place 1 st on all
rem ndls. Third size: Place 1 st on
each of the first 5 ndls, [place 2 sts
on next ndl, and 1 st on each of the
next 2 ndls] to last 5 ndls, place 1st
on each of the last 5 ndls. Fourth
size: [Place 1 st on each of the first
2 ndls and 2 sts on next ndl] to end.
K 1 row loosely, cast off.
Discard WY.

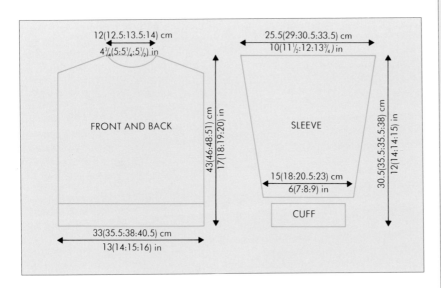

COLLAR
Push 111(113:115:117) ndls to WP. Set machine for K1 P1 rib. With C, cast on selvedge. TD MT –1 RC 000. Rib 30 rows, hook up to main bed (see note). Cast off.

DIAGONAL RIDGES
Lock card 2 on row 1. Push 20 ndls to WP. Either follow chart shown, or place ridges as you wish in this way. With R/S work facing, and with the welt at the top, fold work diagonally across two squares, placing loops on to the ndls, from one st in from the vertical stripe and 1 st down from the horizontal stripe. The centre 4 sts are picked up where the two stripes cross. Pick up the rem sts evenly between. Set ndls for the first row of patt (see manual). With E in feeder 1/A and F in feeder 2/B, unlock card, K 6 rows. Lock card. Make a small hem by picking up the loops from the first row. Cast off.

DESIGNER TIP:
The graph is simply a guide. Feel free to add as many or as few creepies and crawlies as you wish - in any formation.

MAKING UP
If you have joined shoulders, sleeves and collar on the machine sew sleeve and side seams. Knot cords. If you are sewing up garment by hand, join shoulders with a flat seam, sew in sleeves to the markers, sew cast off edge of collar around neckline. Sew sleeve and side seams. Knot cords. Press according to instructions on the ball band and keep one ball band for washing instructions.

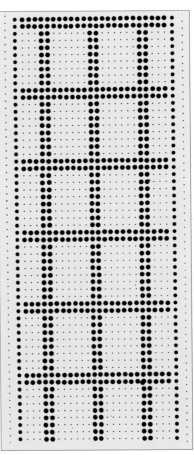

CARD 1

CARD 2

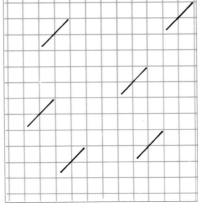

Centre
98 sts

WELT   WELT

Diagram for placing diagonal ridges on front and back

EARL GREY

MACHINE
Standard Gauge 24 st punchcard.

MATERIALS
Jaeger Alpaca 4 ply. 50 gm balls.
F 6(7:7:8) balls No: 320
E 6(6:6:7) balls No: 149
D 2(2:2:3) balls No: 142
C 1(1:1:2) balls No: 312
G 1 ball No: 343

TENSION
Main Tension Dial approx No: 8
33 sts and 37 rows – 10 cm (4 in)
square, measured over pattern.

MEASUREMENTS
To fit chest:
96.5(101.5:106.5:112) cm
38(40:42:44) in
Actual size:
106.5(112:117:122) cm
42(44:46:48) in
Length:
63.5(66:66:68.5) cm
25(26:26:27) in
Sleeve length:
48(48:48:52) cm
19(19:19:20½) in

ABBREVIATIONS
(see page 7)

NOTES
Photographed garment knitted to
third size.
NB: Knit side is right side.
Punch card illustrated before
starting to knit.

PATTERN
With the first colour in feeder 1/A
and the second colour in feeder
2/B, K 12 rows F/E, 2 rows C/G,
12 rows F/E, 6 rows D/F, 2 rows
C/G, 6 rows D/F.
These 40 rows form pattern.

BACK
Lock card on row 1.
NB: Mark each end of row
118(122:118:122) with WY.
Push 173(181:189:197) ndls to
WP. Set machine for K1 P1 rib.
With E, cast on selvedge. TD MT –3
RC 000. Rib 30 rows. Hook up to
main bed, inc 1 st on L to centre
work. TD MT RC 000. K 1 row,
setting carr for patt. Unlock card, K
in patt to RC 205(213:213:221). K
a few rows with WY and remove
from machine.

FRONT
Work as back to RC 115. Remove
from machine the centre 48 sts and
all rem sts on opp side to carr.
(Card row 55). On first side cont in
patt to RC 205(213:213:221). Slip
sts on to WY and remove from
machine. Replace sts from rem
front on to machine over the same
ndls as before. Reset card and ndls.
Place carr at centre front. Cast off
the first 48 sts, unlock card and
work to match first side. Slip sts
on to WY and remove from
machine.
  JOIN SHOULDERS: With R/S
back facing, place last row on to
machine. With W/S front facing,
place shoulder sts on top of back
shoulder sts, discarding WY. Carr L.
TD 10. K1 row across all sts.
  Cast off.

SLEEVES
Lock card on row 1.
Push 92(98:106:114) ndls to WP.
With WY, cast on and K a few rows.
Change to E. TD MT RC 000. K 1 row,
setting machine for patt. Unlock card
and cont in patt, shaping sides by inc
1 st each end of 4th and every foll
4th row to RC 146(146:146:160).
162(168:176:184) sts (see note).
Cast off.

CUFFS
Push 69(69:71:73) ndls to WP. Set
machine for K1 P1 rib. With E, cast
on selvedge. TD MT –3 RC 000. Rib
30 rows. Hook up to main bed.
With W/S sleeve facing, place first
row on top of cuff sts as follows:
First size: * Place 1 st on each of the
first 2 ndls and 2 sts on next ndl *.
Rep from * to *. Second size: Place
2 sts on each of the first 5 ndls, rep
from * to * on first size, then place 2
sts on each of the last 4 ndls. Third
size: Place 2 sts on each of the first
9 ndls, rep from * to * on first size,
then place 2 sts on each of the last
9 ndls. Fourth size: Place 2 sts on
each of the first 13 ndls, rep from *
to * on first size, then place 2 sts on
each of the last 13 ndls. K 1 row
loosely by hand. Cast off.

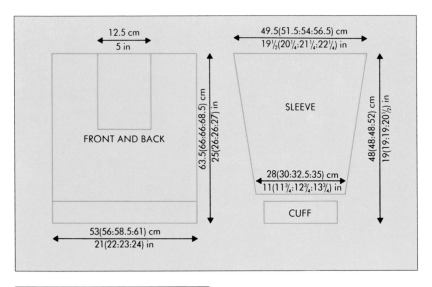

12.5 cm
5 in

49.5(51.5:54:56.5) cm
19½(20¼:21¼:22¼) in

FRONT AND BACK

SLEEVE

63.5(66:66:68.5) cm
25(26:26:27) in

48(48:48:52) cm
19(19:19:20½) in

28(30:32.5:35) cm
11(11¾:12¾:13¾) in

CUFF

53(56:58.5:61) cm
21(22:23:24) in

COLLAR
Push 161(171:171:181) ndls to
WP. Set machine for K1 P1 rib.
With E, cast on selvedge. TD MT –3
RC 000. Rib 60 rows. Cast off.
Repeat using F.

MAKING UP
If you have not joined sleeves to
body on machine, then sew in to
markers. Sew sleeve and side
seams. Sew cast off edge of collar
from centre back neck down side of
neck. Sew E collar on to left side of
neck and F on to right side of neck.
Overlap and sew on to cast off sts.
Sew centre back collar seam. Press
according to instructions on the ball
band and keep one ball band for
washing instructions.

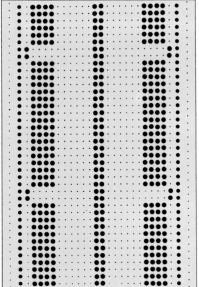

DESIGNER TIP:
When you have
completed the black and
red rows, don't cut the
yarns. Take them out of
the carriage and put
them to one side ready
for use on the next
repeat.

LIST OF STOCKISTS

For local stocklists in each country, please contact the manufacturers below:

GREAT BRITAIN

Argyll Wools Ltd.,
P.O.Box 15,
Priestley Mills,
Pudsey,
W. Yorks. LS28 9LT

Hayfield Textiles Ltd.,
Hayfield Mills,
Glusburn,
North Keighley,
West Yorks. BD20 8QP

Jaeger,
McMullen Rd.,
Darlington,
Co Durham DL1 1YQ.

Lister,
George Lee & Sons Ltd.,
Whiteoak Mills,
Westgate,
Wakefield
W. Yorks. WF2 9SF

Patons,
Patons and Baldwins Ltd.,
McMullen Rd.,
Darlington
Co. Durham DL1 1YQ

Phildar,
4 Gambrel Road,
Westgate Industrial Estate,
Northampton. NN5 5NS

Pingouin,
French Wools Ltd.,
7 — 11 Lexington St,
London W1R 4BU

Rowan Yarns Ltd.,
Green Lane Mill,
Huddersfield
W. Yorks. HD7 1RW

Sirdar PLC,
Flanshaw Lane,
Alverthorpe,
Wakefield,
W. Yorks. WF2 9ND

Silverknit,
Calverton Road,
Nottingham.

Sunbeam,
Crawshaw Mills,
Robin Lane,
Pudsey,
W. Yorks. LS28 7BS.

Twilleys,
H.G.Twilley Ltd.,
Roman Mill,
Stamford,
Lincs. PE9 1BG

AUSTRALIA

Hayfield Textiles Ltd.,
Panda Yarns, (International) Ltd.,
17-27 Brunswick Road,
East Brunswick,
Victoria 3057.

Patons,
Coats and Patons Australia Ltd.,
P.O. Box 110,
Ferntree Gully Road,
Mount Waverley,
Victoria 3149.

Pingouin,
C. Sullivan PTY Ltd.,
3 Ralph Avenue,
Alexandria, NSW 2015.

Sirdar,
Sirdar (Australia) PTY Ltd.,
P.O. Box 110,
Mt. Waverley,
Victoria 3149.

Twilleys,
Panda Yarns, (International) Ltd.,
17-27 Brunswick Road,
East Brunswick,
Victoria 3057.

Rowan,
Sunspun Enterprises, PTY
195 Canterbury Road,
Canterbury 3126.

Jaeger,
Coats Patons Australia Ltd.,
P.O. Box 110
Ferntree
Gully Road,
Victoria 3149.

CANADA

Argyll Wools Ltd,
Estelle Designs and Sales Ltd,
1135 Queen Street East,
Toronto.

Hayfield Textiles Ltd.,
Craftsmen Distributors Inc.,
P.O. Box 374,
Abbottsford,
British Colombia,
V25 4NJ.

Lister-Lee Yarn Plus,
120/5726 Burleigh Cres,
Calgary,
Alberta.

Patons,
Patons and Baldwins Inc.,
1001 Roselawn Ave,
Toronto,
Ontario M6B 1B8.

Jaeger,
(As Patons address above)

Phildar,
Phildar Ltd.,
6200 Est Boulevard H Bourassa,
Montreal Nord,
H1G 5 X3.

Rowan,
Estelle,
38 Continental Place,
Scarborough,
Ontario,
M1R 2T4 Canada.

Pingouin,
Promafil Canada,
300 Laurentian Boulevard,
Suite 100,
Ville St. Laurent,
Quebec, H4M 2L4.

Sirdar,
Diamond Yarn Corp,
9697 St. Laurence Boulevard,
Montreal,
Quebec.

Sunbeam
Estelle Designs and Sales Ltd.,
38, Continental Place,
Scarborough,
Ontario M1R 2T4.

UNITED STATES
Hayfield Textiles Ltd.,
Shepherd Wools Inc.,
711 Johnson Avenue,
Blain, Washington 98230. USA.

Patons, Susan Bates Inc.,
212 Middlesex Avenue,
Route 9A, Chester, Connecticutt,
06412. USA.

Jaeger,
(As Patons address above)

Pingouin,
M. Oliver Prouvost Promafil Corp,
P.O. Box 100,
Jamestown,
South Carolina.

Rowan Yarns,
Westminster Trading,
5 Northern Boulevard,
Amherst,
New Hampshire, 03031.

Sirdar,
Kendex Corp,
P.O. Box 1909
616 Fitch Avenue,
Moorpark
California, 93021.

Sunbeam,
Pirates Cove,
P.O. Box 57,
Babylon,
New York
11702.

SOUTH AFRICA
Patons,
Patons and Baldwins South Africa
PTY Ltd.,
P.O. Box 33,
Randfontein 1760
Transvaal.

Sirdar and Jaeger,
(As Patons address above)

Sunbeam,
MR. C. Rayner,
Brasch Hobby,
57, La Rochelle Road,
Trojan,
Johannesburg.

Pingouin,
Mr. Peter Grobler Saprotex,
Saprotex International PTY Ltd.,
P.O. Box 306,
New Germany 3620.

Twilleys,
F.W. Nyman & Co. Ltd.,
P.O. Box 4386,
Johannesburg 2000.

NEW ZEALAND
Patons
Coats Patons New Zealand Ltd.,
263, Tirakau Drive,
Pakuranga,
Auckland.

Jaeger,
(As Patons address above)

Rowan Yarns,
Creative Fashion Centre,
PO Box 45083,
Epuni Railway,
Lower Hutt.

Sirdar
Alliance Textiles,
P.O. Box 2500,
106 Parnell Road,
Auckland.

▮NDEX

NB The words "see note" in patterns refer to the guidance notes on pages 9–17 of the Introduction

ACKNOWLEDGMENTS

The author would like to thank the knitters who worked so hard to finish the sweaters in time for photography; Mary Elliott, who for years has worked for me on some very complicated designs with humour and an ability to get there in the end; Maureen Carr, who stepped in when most needed and who, with Mary, completed 27 of the 31 garments in the book; Ron and Myrtle Feldwick, and Gwen Knott.

The author and publishers would also like to thank the following people and organisations for their assistance:

Patterns checked by	Mary Smith
Models	Jane Harwood
	Tessa Peters
	Denise Hill
	Matthew Canon
	Billie Lever-Taylor
	Paddy
Make up and Hair	Valerie McDonald

Jousse, and The Hat Shop